DEVOTIONS
FOR
GRANDPARENTS

Books in This Series

By Cecil B. Murphey
  Devotions for Joggers
  Devotions for Calorie Counters
  Devotions for Lovers
  Devotions for Travelers
  Devotions for Worriers
  Devotions for Grandparents
  Devotions for Winners

By Phillip Barnhart
  Devotions for Insomniacs
  Devotions for Patients

By Joan Masters
  Devotions for Nurses

DEVOTIONS
FOR
GRANDPARENTS

Cecil B. Murphey

SPIRE ⬛ BOOKS

Fleming H. Revell Company
Old Tappan, New Jersey

ISBN: 0-8007-8452-9

A Spire Book
Copyright © 1983 Fleming H. Revell Company
All Rights Reserved
Printed in the United States of America

Old men are proud of their grandchildren,
just as boys are proud of their fathers.

Proverbs 17:6 TEV

DEVOTIONS
FOR
GRANDPARENTS

What Is a Grandparent?

> Dear friends, let us love one another, because
> love comes from God. Whoever loves is a child
> of God and knows God.
>
> 1 John 4:7 TEV

Week 1, Day 1

What's a grandparent?

An obvious definition says that a grandparent is a parent whose children have children.

I heard a psychological definition of a grandparent the other day: a grandparent is a uniquely and emotionally involved, part-time parent who is without pressure. That definition fits most grandparents. First, we are those who are part-time parents or as the Latin phrase says, *in loco parentis* ("in place of the parents"). When a grandparent acts in place of a parent, he or she fulfills the role of a parent to the children.

As grandparents, we're part-time parents and so quite different from babysitters. We're different because we're emotionally involved, while babysitters may or may not be. Because of this emotional involvement, we grandparents take the job of caring for our grandchildren more seriously and responsibly than the average babysitter.

On the other hand, we're not usually as objective about the children as an outsider is. We're more likely to be defensive about the way the parents handle the children.

We're also "without pressure." By that, I mean as grandparents we do not have the full responsibility for raising the children. We can enjoy them for a brief time and then hand them back to their parents. Since we're not in charge of the children, we don't have to set goals.

We're not responsible for buying clothes, feeding them, or staying awake all night with a sick infant.

Most of all, being a grandparent provides a unique responsibility for us. As grandparents, we love our children and our children's children. We recognize that God gave them to us to love. As we show affection for our children's offspring, we're reflecting God's love to them. We're teaching them, by the way we treat them, how good God is.

We're also unique in another way. No matter how many friends or teachers a child may have, that child will have a maximum of four grandparents. We represent two of them. We're unique and wonderful in a child's life. Let's thank God for the privilege.

God, thank You that we can love our children and our children's children. As we love them, may they realize that our love comes from You and that we're merely passing it on to them. Amen.

All Things New

Then he took Simon to Jesus. Jesus looked at him and said, "Your name is Simon son of John, but you will be called Cephas." (This is the same as Peter and means "a rock.")
                                                    John 1:42 TEV

Week 1, Day 2

"My wife wishes me to announce," I said from the pulpit one Sunday, "that she has just become a grandmother."

Folks chuckled and someone whispered, "Yes, and she sleeps with a grandfather."

That was the beginning of our becoming grandparents—in many ways the start of an exciting time of life, certainly a whole new phase of life.

So now you're a grandparent. Prior to that time you may have envisioned grandparents as elderly, stooped over, and white-haired. Now you suddenly look at yourself and you don't fit that stereotype; but you're still a grandparent.

All kinds of new things are happening. First of all you have a new name. *Grandparent.*

Getting a new name is in itself a transition. For instance, most women take their husband's name when they marry. In some cultures the husband and wife have a double surname so that when Jim Smith and Alice Jones marry, the last name would become Jones-Smith. In those cases where divorce happens, sometimes the woman takes back her maiden name. There are cases where people legally change their names for various reasons, but at any rate a new name always signifies a change of relationship.

In the Bible, when a person received a new name it signified a drastic change for him. Saul became Paul. Jacob received the name of Israel.

In the New Testament we read of a fisherman named Simon. One day he met Jesus. At that moment of meeting he received a new name, *Peter* (in the Greek, Cephas). The incident signaled more than changing a name. It was Jesus' way of telling Peter he was entering into a whole new relationship.

Being called *Grandma* instead of *Mommy* also signals a drastic change in life.

Among other things, being a grandparent means your child is now grown. That little toddler whose diapers you once changed is now a mature person, changing diapers on his or her own child.

Perhaps one of the best things about being a grandparent is that it is *grand.* It means that as a grandfather I have raised my children. Now it's their turn to raise theirs. It means that I relinquish my authority over them (if I haven't done so already). Now I become more an observer than a doer. Everything changes. Being a grandparent makes me realize life goes on. I'm part of the life-cycle that goes on from generation to generation.

When I look into the eyes of my two grandchildren, it makes me realize how wonderful life can be. It also makes me realize what a great privilege it is to be a grandparent.

Lord God, in my role of grandparent, help me to appreciate this new phase of my life. Help me also to be the best grandparent I'm capable of being. Amen.

Coming of Age

Much later the Lord gave Israel security from their enemies around them. By that time Joshua was very old, so he called all Israel, the elders, leaders, judges, and officers of the people, and said, "I am very old now."

Joshua 23:1, 2 TEV

Week 1, Day 3

"My grandma is old on the outside but very young inside," a nine-year-old boy said to me one Sunday.

I normally wear contact lenses. One evening I had an experience with Danny, my six-year-old grandson. He came to see me and I had my glasses on. He looked at me and said, "Grandpa, you look like an old man with those glasses on."

Both of these experiences remind us of age. We are older. We've lived a good life, full of experiences. We've had our children and now our children are having theirs. We're the grandparents. Instead of being the *now* generation, we're often called the *former* generation. We're no longer young. We're moving up into middle years or even old age.

For some, facing the aging process frightens them. They do everything they can to recapture youth. One of the saddest sights I can think of is the woman who covers her face with what appears to be three inches of makeup base, bright red lipstick, and badly dyed hair. All of these things say she is trying to run away from the reality of age. Men are now catching on to some of the tricks, dyeing their hair or wearing toupees and having hair transplants. I've heard some men are even beginning to wear makeup.

We *are* grandparents and we *are* getting older. As we watch our grandchildren grow, we find constant reminders of our age. When the little ones say to us, "What was it like in the old days?" we are reminded that we're living in a new world. Our skin is wrinkling, our teeth fall out, physical afflictions attack our body—all signs of the aging process.

We can age gracefully if we choose to. If we accept our age and realize that we have already lived the better portion of our life, we can make these remaining years meaningful and significant. Because we're grandparents, and at least middle aged, we know that many of the dreams of our youth are dead. We'll never fulfill them. If we're still part of the work force, we'll probably not advance very much in the next few years. We can use these years to regret the past and mourn over our mistakes.

Or we can make these happy years. One way we make our years happy is by being with our grandchildren as much as possible. We pass on to them our love, our attention and our wisdom. We fix their toys or bake them goodies. Aging doesn't mean that we quit living.

The Bible tells us about Joshua, a great leader and soldier. He led the armies of God into the promised land and overthrew all their enemies. Then great peace came upon the land. Near the end of his life he called the people together and said, "I'm growing old. I'm relinquishing leadership." Shortly afterwards he died.

We don't need to be preoccupied with death and physical illness. Rather, we can rejoice in all the good things that God has given us in our lives. We not only enjoyed our children, but in some way enjoy our grandchildren more. We can take them out, be with them, and then get away from them.

Being a grandparent is a wonderful time of life. We see some of our physical characteristics living on in the new generation. We have the opportunity to teach some of our values and religious commitments. We're in the grand time in life. Let's enjoy being grandparents.

God, thank You that I have lived to see not only my children grown but to see my children's children. Thank You, God, that I'm a grandparent and that I've come of age. Amen.

Who Needs Grandparents?

And he [Jesus] said to them, "Come away by yourselves to a lonely place, and rest a while."

Mark 6:31 RSV

Week 1, Day 4

I don't remember any of my grandparents. All but my father's mother died before I was born, and she died when I was too young to remember her. My parents and older sisters told me stories about her. I always felt cheated because they told me of lovely things she did for them. They often spoke of how much they had enjoyed visiting her.

I never knew a grandparent, but I do remember a man who behaved like one. When I was quite young an older man, a Mr. Lee, lived with us for a while. He was retired, and I recall mostly that Mr. Lee ate a lot of raspberry jam. Every day (or so my memory tells me) he invited us younger children into his room to share his jam. I didn't like raspberry, but I ate it because I enjoyed being with him. He was always kind and often let me sit on his knee.

I never knew a grandfather, but in many ways Mr. Lee was like one because I needed him. He filled a void in my life.

Who needs grandparents? Everybody needs a grandparent—whether a biological one or purely an emotional one. Mr. Lee always had time for me. We were a family of seven children, and I was number five. My mother was busy, and the older ones didn't always have time for me. I remember that any time I went to see Mr. Lee he had time to listen. He heard many of my childhood fears and secrets.

Everyone needs someone who will listen, someplace to go where he or she can simply rest and get away from the hassles and problems of life. That's one function grandparents can serve. We can take time to enjoy children, to listen to them, to let them tell us their problems or share their joys. We can be there when they need to get away from their routine.

In the same way, Jesus and His disciples went away from time to time. They relaxed and separated themselves from the hassle of daily living. They needed a change of pace and of environment. Everyone needs an opportunity to get away from the routine and daily grind of life.

As grandparents, we can offer that very change of pace to our grandchildren.

Who needs a grandparent? *Every child.*

Lord God, thank You that I'm a grandparent and that I can be that person and provide the place where a child can come, relax, and get away from the regular routine of life. Amen.

Who Needs Grandchildren?

> Generations come and generations go, but the
> world stays just the same.
>
> Ecclesiastes 1:4 TEV

Week 1, Day 5

Like most parents, we loved our children and enjoyed
watching them grow. We cried with them when they
were hurt, felt bad when they did something wrong, and
regretted their mistakes. As I've talked to parents who
are empty nesters and grandparents, one of the things
we all say is that somehow our children grew up too fast.

Strange, because I can remember, when my children
were preschoolers, I thought, "Oh, if they'd only get out
of this stage and into school." As parents, there's always
a sense in which we're looking for our children to grow
up and to fulfill the plans and aims we have for them
and that they have for themselves. And then one day we
realize they are grown and our children are gone from
our homes, busy raising their own families.

So who needs grandchildren? We do. It's our chance
to live again through the little ones, to watch and grow
and go through the stages of life that our own children
went through. Now we can love them and care about
them, but relax a little more. We know we did a pretty
good job in raising our own children; now we can relax a
little as we watch our children's children grow.

I have two grandsons. The older is seven and the
younger two. Already they're growing up too fast. While
I want to see them mature, at the same time there's a de-
sire to keep them young and dependent. I want them to
stay cuddly and soft. But like my own children, they're
growing up and one day they'll have their children also.

Who needs grandchildren? I do. I need to see new life. I need to hold little ones. I need to help little ones learn to hold a spoon, to help them repeat words plainly, to take their hand when they're learning to walk.

Who needs grandchildren? I do. I need them to remind me that life goes on. That not only is life eternal for me with Jesus Christ, but there's a sense in which the eternal life flows on through my children to their children and to the next generation. The life and love of God flows on through us. God is continuing His beautiful world by creating people with unique personalities and talents.

Who needs grandchildren? I do. They keep me young, alert, and alive and remind me that I'm still part of God's wonderful creation. Being with my grandchildren keeps before me the realization that I have a purpose in life. I not only have people to love, but I also have people who love me.

God, thank You for grandchildren. We bestow so much love upon them and we pray for only the best in life, even as we prayed for our own children. Thank You for them. Amen.

At the Appointed Time

> Everything that happens in this world happens
> at the time God chooses. He sets the time for
> birth and the time for death. . . .
>
> Ecclesiastes 3:1, 2 TEV

Week 1, Day 6

"But I don't want to be a grandmother," she said. "I'm too young."

Marian heard Lil say those words and she smiled. "Being a grandmother doesn't mean you're getting older; it just means you're going to be able to enjoy life a lot more."

Being a grandparent offers us a lot of privileges. First, we're going to be able to do things that we couldn't do before.

Second, being a grandparent also enables us to establish a closer and warmer relationship with our own adult children than we've known for a long time. The birth of a child gives us an opportunity to get close to our own children again.

I have been aware that even though I felt close to my daughters when they were younger, as they got older our relationship changed. In their teens, we drew apart. After they married and became parents, it seemed as though my daughters entered into an entirely new relationship with me. Now we are able to love and appreciate each other on an adult level. We have established a deeper relationship.

Third, I've discovered that grandchildren make us feel young again instead of older. Something about being close to those youngsters as they grow up keeps us alert. As we listen to them question, talk, and wonder at the world we live in, it makes us think young again. It certainly keeps us from shuffling along on the sidelines of life as we grow older.

One day I expect to be completely gray and terribly wrinkled. But I have a vision in my mind, a vision of walking down a sidewalk or a road with a young child's hand in mine. I think that's what being a grandparent does. It means we're enjoying life and seeing through a child's eyes again.

Fourth, we have the satisfaction of teaching our grandchildren things that are going to stay with them the rest of their lives. The Apostle Paul referred to the faith of Timothy's mother as well as his grandmother, meaning that both of them had taught him well. I have a close friend, Vicki, who says her grandmother practically raised her and in many ways was more of a mother to her than her own parent.

As we love our grandchildren and spend time with

them, many of them are going to want to be like us. I remember when then five-year-old Danny said to me, "I want to be a preacher like you when I grow up."

Will Danny become a preacher? I don't know and it doesn't matter. The point is that even in his young life he had picked up the influence of his grandfather. I like to believe that I have taught him good things about life and that most of all I have taught him about Jesus Christ's love for him.

Being a grandparent provides a second chance for us. We can pass on lessons of life we've learned through experience, often through heartache and disappointment. We can pass on our wisdom. Because of surviving this long in life, we can teach a great deal about grace, forgiveness, and love.

As the Book of Ecclesiastes says, everything that happens in this world happens at the time God chooses. God has appointed a time for us to be grandparents. This time of grandparenting can be one of the best periods of our whole life.

God, thank You that I'm a grandparent. Thank You for the privileges that I have at this wonderful season of my life. Amen.

Getting Older

I am an old man now; I have lived a long time,
but I have never seen a good man abandoned
by the Lord or his children begging for food.
                                    Psalms 37:25 TEV

Week 1, Day 7

The attractive brunette sat before me and began talking about her depression. Finally she burst into tears. "I'm going to be a grandmother and I hate it."

As the details poured out, she really wasn't talking about being a grandmother—she was afraid of getting old. Facing the fact of being a grandparent made her accept the fact that she was no longer a young person.

No matter at what age we become grandparents, the arrival of that first grandchild forces us to the inescapable fact: we are getting older. It doesn't matter whether our first grandchild was born when we were thirty-seven or fifty-five; we are getting older. To those of us who have already come to terms psychologically with aging, becoming a grandparent can be a fulfilling experience.

I saw this happen with my wife. She never thought much about getting older simply because she was becoming a grandparent. She had already come to terms with the fact that she was middle-aged. Being a grandparent was the next fulfilling step for her. Others avoid facing their age, and becoming a grandparent provokes a lot of defensive reactions.

The reaction we have in becoming a grandparent often amplifies where we are in our life. Most of us go through mid-life crisis somewhere between the ages of forty and fifty. In women this usually coincides with menopause. With men it happens somewhere between forty-five and fifty.

We're taught from childhood to look ahead as if our future were endless. When the mid-life crisis comes we're suddenly forced to see that the future is not endless. We grapple with the fact that of the hundreds of options we once had, most of them are now gone. We can no longer make the type of career decisions at forty-five that we could still make at twenty-five.

Until the reality of mid-life hits us, we work at our jobs, we raise our children, we plan for the future. Now for perhaps the first time we're forced to look inward and raise questions. What does my work mean to me? Am I really fulfilled? Is my marriage bringing me true happiness? What do my children mean to me? What is the meaning of life? Is this all there is?

Accepting the reality of middle age doesn't come easy for all of us, particularly for those of us who look five or ten years younger or act considerably younger.

Being a grandparent may be an experience like the brunette who sat before me. She had to confront an undeniable reality: she was getting older.

One thing we can do to help ourselves is make statements such as the one found in the psalm: I am old, once I was young. By saying those words to ourselves they remind us of our advancing age and enable us to accept the implications of age. We *are* getting older, and grandchildren provide one of the joys of our advancing years.

God, help me not only accept the fact that I'm no longer young. Help me also accept the fact that now I can enjoy my grandchildren. Amen.

Openness

Love must be completely sincere.
Romans 12:9 TEV

Week 2, Day 1

"Grandpa, why do you always give me long answers when I ask short questions?"

I heard a boy ask that question once. I chuckled inside. I had observed that he asked a very simple question, and the grandfather went on for five minutes giving an answer.

If we really want to be open and get rid of roadblocks in our relationship with grandchildren, here's one of the first rules: be brief when we respond. Most adults are much too long-winded with children. They ask a simple question and want just as simple and as short an answer.

Here are other ways to open the communication and let the children know that we are attempting to talk and to listen. Number two: let your body send the message to your child that you are actively listening. Don't dust or stare at the TV or continue to mend a broken chair. That child knows that he or she is out of your main focus of attention, and the conversation fades away. When we're talking to our grandchild, we do best if we maintain an eye-to-eye contact that lets the child know we're concentrating on what's being said.

Number three: use the feedback technique. If Julie is talking about her problem at school and starts giving you details, one way you show Julie you're listening is to feed back some of what she said—the important words or phrases—to let her know that you've been listening.

Number four: inject comments that keeps the child talking. We can say things such as, "Well, what happened next?" or "She really said that, huh?" These comments show the child that you're listening and are waiting for the next part of the story or situation. That child is aware that you are with her/him.

Number five: talk to one child at a time. We have plenty of opportunities to talk to more than one of our grandchildren at social occasions such as dinner. The children don't usually open up as readily when another person is present. Strive for one-to-one conversations. That's when we have the deepest level of communication. One way to achieve this is to take each of the grandchildren out for a meal or an occasional trip, just the two of you or both grandparents and the single child. Let the child know that he/she is special, important, and has your time and attention.

Number six: show respect. Children have a lot less information about the world than we do, but they still have their own points of view. Often adults cut them off because of their immature reasoning or their lack of proper perception and just simply say things like, "That's silly." It may sound silly to an adult, but it may be quite serious to the child.

Number seven: we must disclose ourselves as real people with human feelings and weaknesses. Young children picture their parents and grandparents as powerful and superior. One time my grandson Danny said, "Grandpa, you know everything, don't you?"

We help these children by showing them that we have fears, worries, and times of indecision just as they do. Sometimes children don't have parents and grandparents who reveal fears and weaknesses. When they have problems come up in their life, they have difficulty coping. We do our children a favor by showing them that we're only human after all.

There's no way that we can guarantee open communication with our grandchildren. Most of all, of course, we need to love them and love them sincerely.

One final thing: never hesitate to apologize. When we're wrong, when we've made a promise we haven't been able to keep, when we've said something that we regret, apologize. Let the children see the real grandparent—an imperfect human.

Holy Father, help me to have a loving relationship with my grandchildren. Let our love for each other be sincere and open, just as I want the relationship between You and me to be more open all the time. Amen.

Roadblocks

Thoughtless words can wound as deeply as any sword, but wisely spoken words can heal.
Proverbs 12:18 TEV

Week 2, Day 2

"My teacher, Mrs. Rice, is as ugly as a gorilla," grandson John says one day.

"John, that's no way to talk about your teacher."

When we answer like that, we have been judgmental. John wants our approval, and when we're judgmental we discourage him from making other comments for fear that they too might possibly draw critical responses from us. By talking to our children and grandchildren this way, we may cut off future conversations about things deeply important to them. For instance, fear of disapproval is one reason why parents and children talk so little on the subject of sex. Children quickly sense it's a foreign subject and stay away from it. If we want to encourage our grandchildren to talk freely, we need to avoid making shocked or negative responses to them.

We set up all kinds of roadblocks in our relationship to our grandchildren. I want to point out a few others.

We deny our grandchild's feelings. We do this by saying, "You aren't still bothered about that problem, are you?" Obviously if the child wasn't still bothered by it, he/she would not continue to talk about it. To us it may be a small problem, but to the child it may be immensely large.

"Oh, don't worry, honey. Things will work out fine." That's a glib reassurance. We're not being honest unless we're really sure things are going to work out. Sometimes we throw easy sentences at the children. What happens if it doesn't work out?

I remember one time my own daughter was treated unfairly in school. While I felt incensed inside I simply said to her, "You know, that's the way life is. Everything doesn't come out even and right." I was trying to say to her, everything isn't always all right, sometimes things don't work out well. At the same time I tried to assure her that it wasn't going to spoil her entire world. She got through the experience quite well.

Sometimes we try to solve the children's problems by offering them solutions. Unconsciously we say, "Listen, here's what I'd do the next time the situation comes up." We need to remind ourselves that we're not that child and our solution may not fit the situation. Our grandchildren may not want us to solve their problem. We do more for them by listening and letting them work it out themselves. We won't always be there to solve all of life's problems for them.

We tend to lecture. When my daughter explained about the trouble with her teacher I could have said,

"Well, everyone has trouble with her teacher. I remember when I was in third grade." What we forget is this is not my third grade and never can be. My third grade and my daughter's third grade were at least a generation apart.

Sometimes we attack. We do this by saying, "Okay, now what did you do to make your brother angry?" We act as if we're omniscient and we know exactly who's to blame. We pin the child down, assuming the problems solve themselves.

We also moralize. That is, we tell our child what he/she ought to do. "You need to go over to Janice and tell her you're sorry. Make up and forget all this ever happened." Let her decide when it's time to make up with Janice. We can talk to her about the principle of forgiveness, but let her make up her own mind, or when and if she ought to apologize.

We threaten, too. This is a favorite method of many grandparents. "Look, I'm telling you for the last time, if you say that once more I'll smack your face." We may get the behavior at that moment. But threats do little to change future conduct, although parents and grandparents never seem weary of trying this approach.

Finally, we play psychiatrist. "Anne, you're just insecure, and so you're constantly butting in to gain attention." Most of us don't have seven years of psychoanalytical training, and we can't figure out other people's motives. We sometimes do a lot of harm with this kind of roadblock.

Because we're grandparents who love our offspring, we want to do away with every form of communication hindrance. Skim back over these nine roadblocks I've mentioned. Pray over each one. Ask, "Lord, am I guilty of violating this one?" And if so, ask God's help. Ask Him to help you eliminate this roadblock.

Heavenly Father, I want no roadblocks in the relationship with my grandchildren. Help me to eliminate them all and replace these roadblocks with a greater depth of love. Amen.

When Divorce Strikes

Be kind and tender-hearted to one another,
and forgive one another, as God has forgiven
you through Christ.

Ephesians 4:32 TEV

Week 2, Day 3

Here are a few statistics: approximately four out of ten
children born in the 1970s will live in a single-parent
home during part of their childhood. One out of every
eight children in America now lives in a single-parent
home. Less than 10 percent of the American population
lives in what we call the typical American situation—
one with a breadwinner father, a homemaker mother,
and children.

These are today's facts. Probably the most frightening
is the divorce rate. It shows no inclination toward de-
clining. We will probably see even more single-parent
families in the future. If our daughter or son goes
through a divorce, it will be one of the most traumatic
events of their lives. Probably neither of them have been
through it before and won't have the faintest idea what
to expect. As someone said, "The divorce jungle is filled
with venomous snakes and dangerous animals as well as
banditos [lawyers], and we've had no training to protect
ourselves against any of these beasts."

How does this affect us as grandparents? When we
find out our child is getting a divorce, we're usually
upset. What's the right thing to do?

One couple I know and admire very much said to
both the son-in-law and the daughter, "We're sorry
things are not working out, but we're not going to take
sides because we love you both. We're here to support

either of you or both of you if we can."

Not every divorcing couple gets that kind of emotional support from grandparents. They can be a great help in a time of crisis.

People can stop being married to each other, but they never stop being parents to their children. It's in our grandchildren's best interests for their father and mother, though divorced, to remain as amicable as possible. It doesn't do our children any good through the years to be exposed to the spectacle of the parents' hatred for each other. It doesn't help when we spew out our venom toward our ex-daughter-in-law.

Our child and our grandchildren go through a time of mourning when divorce comes. For instance, if their father died, the children and the mother would need to go through a period of grief. Even though divorce may not be an actual death, it is the psychological death of a family, and there will be mourning.

In divorce there may be relief that there is no longer any fighting. It may be relief that now husband and wife can begin to have peace and some direction in life. Even so, there's usually mourning involved. Particularly we need to consider that the children generally love both parents.

When our child divorces, as grandparents we probably won't be able to remain truly neutral and to treat both sides alike. Even if we feel deeply that one person is wrong and deserves the blame, we need to remind ourselves that everyone sees only the outside of a marriage. We really cannot know what's going on in the psychological interior of the relationship. As grandparents, the best thing we can do is keep quiet. We have no idea how much harm we can do ourselves, the parents *and* the grandchildren by taking sides. Sometimes grandparents feel the need to swing their weight around in such situations and learn only too late they really are making a mistake.

Even when we feel our son's ex-wife is completely wrong, we can teach our children and grandchildren a great deal about being a Christian and about God's love by our attitude. We can maintain an attitude of kindness and forgiveness. We can remind ourselves that no human being is ever perfect. It takes two people to make a good marriage; it also takes two people to ruin a good marriage. No one is ever completely faultless. By word, by actions, and certainly by example, we can teach our children and grandchildren how to be kind and tender-hearted and above all to "forgive one another, as God has forgiven you through Christ."

Forgiving God, help me not to take sides when there are problems such as divorce in the family. Help me to be loving and forgiving toward all the parties involved. Amen.

When Children Face Death

Everyone must die once.
Hebrews 9:27 TEV

Week 2, Day 4

"Why is Mommy in the hospital?" four-year-old Danny asked me one day.

"Because she's sick. She's having her tonsils taken out," I answered.

Danny, not understanding hospitals or tonsils, said to me, "Is she going to die?"

"No," I said. "Mommy is sick and soon she will be well. In fact, she'll be home either tomorrow or the next day."

My four-year-old grandson apparently thought that going to the hospital meant his mother was going to die. He may have picked that up from television or from somewhere else. At four years old I'm not sure he even understood what death means. But somewhere along the line children do face death.

They sometimes face it when someone close to them is in the hospital. Today most people do die in the hospital, and this can be a source of great trauma.

Because we're Christian grandparents, one of the things we can do, as the opportunity presents itself, is to teach our children and grandchildren about death.

We can avoid false and sentimental statements when death occurs—statements such as, "God needed another angel in heaven." Death is a reality which people encounter. We don't have to have all the answers.

We can explain in a very simple way to a young child, "Your Aunt Rose is going away; she won't be coming back. She's going to be living with God and we won't see her again." For young children that's usually enough of an answer.

Sometimes they'll ask what it feels like to die and we can give them answers on their level, such as to say, "There is no feeling."

One of the best things I've found when talking to children about death is to use an image which is found in the Bible. The Bible frequently compares death to sleep. When you're asleep, you're unaware of anything going on around you.

One nine-year-old child was quite distraught when his grandfather died. I explained to him that his grandfather had been in a lot of pain, which the boy knew, but now he was dead and that was like being asleep. He was never going to feel pain again. "When he wakes up he will be with God."

That nine-year-old boy thought about my words for a minute and said, "Oh, that's good. I just don't want Grandpa to hurt anymore."

Children usually accept death more realistically than we give them credit for. We make a great deal of death because we have greater emotional attachments and we know adult patterns of grieving. Often children accept death matter of factly. If we impose upon them the need to go through much crying and mourning, we may give them a false idea of death.

Death is sad to those who are left because they miss a

loved one, but to those who die, especially those who die
in Christ, death is a state of blessedness. As grandparents, we have wonderful opportunities to teach our children through the death of a pet, a relative or a friend.

We can teach our grandchildren not to be afraid of
death because God is with us even in the darkest hours
of life and He never leaves us—not even in death.

*Loving Lord, as I face the idea of death with my grand-
children, help me to give them a healthy attitude and understanding. Help them to understand, and me as well,
that death is not an end, it's only a transition from one
phase of life to another. Amen.*

Beddy-Bye

You will not be afraid when you go to bed, and
you will sleep soundly through the night.
                                    Proverbs 3:24 TEV

Week 2, Day 5

"But I'm not sleepy, Grandpa. Let me stay up just a
little bit longer."

As long as I've been taking care of my grandson
Danny, on those rare occasions when he spends the
night and as long as he's been able to talk, he's always
asked to stay up a little later.

As grandparents we're apt to give in and not be quite
as strict sometimes as the parents. Yet children need
their sleep, and we need to make certain that they get it.

When our grandchildren stay with us, we need to
know their bedtime and then to enforce it. Summer and
weekend bedtimes may vary from school bedtimes, but
don't trust grandchildren to tell us the true time. Ask the
parents.

Don't expect children to go gently into that good

night. Bedtime is a ritual for most children, especially young ones. It's a time when we can pray with them, hug them, and perhaps even read them a Bible story. But that doesn't mean it's always an easy time.

Children can think of a dozen reasons for not sleeping. "I want a drink of water." "I have to go to the bathroom." "I left my shoes by the TV set. Can I get up and get them?"

Bedtime can be a beautiful ritual if both child and grandparent know what to expect. One of the things I find helped me both as a parent and a grandparent is to play quietly for a few minutes with the children, perhaps even rock them.

As my children got to be four and five years of age, I discovered it was easier to deal with them if I gave them choices. Rather than ask, "Do you want to go to bed or stay up?" I gave them choices such as "Do you want to walk into the bedroom or would you like me to carry you?"

Another time it would be, "Would you like to crawl into the bedroom or would you like to go hippity-hop?" My children played this game for a long time. They eventually reached the age when my older daughter finally said, "Daddy, it doesn't matter which way I choose, you're still going to make me go to bed, aren't you?" And I said, "Yes."

After that I stopped giving her options, simply informing her that it was bedtime and that I cared about her health and felt she needed to sleep.

For many grandparents, putting the children to bed is a hassle that many of them don't want to deal with. It can be made simpler by making sure the children know what you expect of them and as a grandparent holding the line. Hassles can often be eliminated by such a simple thing as leaving a light on or making sure the child has a particular toy. But if 8:30 is the bedtime, as responsible grandparents we make certain that the child is in bed by 8:30.

Another possibility to help grandchildren get to sleep is to say, "I'll sit here and read a few minutes until you drift off to sleep." Or, "I'll sing a few songs to you, but I want you to lie quietly with your eyes closed."

It takes some children longer to fall asleep than others. But whether or not the child falls asleep easily the child is in bed, and as good grandparents we allow no reasons for getting up again. We are doing this because we are establishing patterns. We want the child to get enough sleep. We want the child to be refreshed for the next day.

The psalmist tells us that God gives sleep to His beloved. We know that our grandchildren are going to wake up refreshed and ready for the morning.

God, let the ritual of putting our grandchildren to sleep be a meaningful experience when we can speak to them of love. May it be a meaningful time rather than a hassle. Amen.

Setting the Rules

> "My son, pay attention when the Lord corrects you, and do not be discouraged when he rebukes you. Because the Lord corrects everyone he loves and punishes everyone he accepts as a son."
>
> Hebrews 12:5, 6 TEV

Week 2, Day 6

Some mothers are not very good disciplinarians. They back off with, "Wait until your father gets home." This can make the child fear Dad because when Dad comes home, the child expects to get spanked.

Unfortunately, in many homes loving correction is not taught. Rules are not spelled out and therefore not understood. This can cause serious family squabbles.

Grandparents can be helpful in raising grandchildren by having rules in their home. When grandchildren come, they know exactly what they can or can't do.

In our home, for instance, we have a toy box in one room. Our grandchildren know that when they visit they may take any of the toys out of the box. They also know they do not leave until they have replaced all the toys. This was a rule we established when my first grandson was quite young, and it's never a point of debate.

To make life easier for yourself and for the grandchildren I offer six suggestions. (1) Set the rules as early as possible. Make them clear, simple, and easy to understand. If the children are to be punished for ignoring the rules, they need to know in advance. (2) If you have a lot of grandchildren and they can read, type out or Xerox copies of the house rules. Tack them on a bathroom wall or the outside of the refrigerator. One grandmother I know has little signs hanging up. In the bathroom, for instance, it says, "We rinse our tub after using." In the room she reserves for grandchildren, she has taped these words, "Did you make your bed?" They are little reminders and the children are expected to obey. (3) As grandparents we have the authority to punish those who disobey, but make sure that the punishment suits the crime and that no child suffers or benefits from favoritism. (4) Be sure your rules are fair. Don't make rules merely for your convenience as a grandparent, but set the kind of rules that enable the household to run more smoothly and more cooperatively. (5) Work with the parents of the children so they know as well as the children what you expect. This does not mean that you must conform to the same rules that the children have in their own home. Children are amazingly versatile in adapting to new situations. Because we have different standards about discipline, most of our children understand our position as long as it's made clear. (6) Explain all this to the children. Let them know that you're doing this so that we can avoid hassles and problems later on. "This is what we expect," you can say. "We love you and we

want your time here to be as happy as possible and not
have to have a lot of arguing going on." Most children
can understand, even though they may need to be reminded from time to time.

As we teach our grandchildren that we have rules in
our home, they understand and respect them. We also
teach them that there are rules in the world, in schools,
in public places; we're helping them not only to be fine
Christians but good citizens of the land. We're teaching
them that rules are expected to be obeyed and that those
who break the rules must be punished.

*Heavenly Father, give me wisdom in setting up rules when
my grandchildren visit. Let them be fair. Most of all, let
them be loving so we can teach our grandchildren more
about the wonderful love of Jesus Christ which they'll see
reflected in us. Amen.*

The Manipulators

Love is not ill-mannered or selfish or irritable;
love does not keep a record of wrongs.
                              1 Corinthians 13:5 TEV

Week 2, Day 7

I remember a movie I saw which was made in the late
thirties. The elderly father was dying and trying to decide what to do with his enormous wealth. He called his
children and grandchildren before him and rebuked
them for their selfishness.

One of the daughters finally said, "You're right. We're
selfish. Part of it is because you've taught us to be that
way." She concluded her speech with something like
this, "So we've really been good children after all,
haven't we?"

It's easy to see selfishness in other people, especially in

our children or our grandchildren. What we don't realize is that we sometimes have encouraged it, or at least allowed it.

One way we allow selfishness is when children manipulate us. They will manipulate us if they can. That's human nature.

Children have subtle ways of getting what they want. We need to learn as grandparents to be aware of their tricks. For instance, when we refuse to let our grandchildren have an extra dessert the boy says, "But Mom always lets me."

We're being manipulated. Logically Mom does not let him, but if Mom is not present, we have no way to check until it's too late. Instead, we can learn to avoid the manipulation trap. Below are seven typical manipulating statements kids make and some suggested responses:

1. "My daddy says that I only have to eat *raw* carrots."
2. "My mommy always lets me go."
3. "My parents said that when I come to your house I can . . ."
4. "My mother never gives me a chance to . . . but I knew that you would let me."
5. "We don't do it that way at our house. Instead we . . ."
6. "You're my favorite. I love you more than Mommy or Daddy or anybody else because you let me . . ."
7. "Daddy says we can't . . . because we don't have the money."

The last two statements seem to be especially made by older children.

No matter how reasonable their request, as grandparents, we need to realize we're being had. We can be had, or we can take control of the situation by informing children that we don't fall for those little tricks and we plan to do it our way.

How do we answer those statements?

1. "That's too bad."
2. "That's too bad."

3. "That's too bad."
4. "That's too bad."
5. "That's too bad."
6. "That's really nice, but that's too bad."
7. "I'll never fall for that. It's too bad you don't have the money."

Once our grandchildren know they can't manipulate us, they tend to stop. We can teach them to love us not because we are strict, but because they know we love them and we want what's best for them. Our relationship can grow even closer.

All-wise God, give me wisdom in dealing with my grandchildren. I don't want to be too hard on them, but neither do I want to be taken advantage of. I want my grandchildren to be loving and I don't want to contribute toward making them selfish individuals. Help me. Amen.

Ego Extensions

When words are many, transgression is not lacking, but he who restrains his lips is prudent.

Proverbs 10:19 RSV

Week 3, Day 1

"Lisa certainly is a beautiful child," I said to her father, Brian.

"Thank you," he answered.

Because I know Brian well, I teasingly added, "Why are you thanking me? I didn't compliment you. Lisa's pretty."

On another occasion the neighbor girl who lived next door had allowed her dog outside. He ran through our garden and trampled all over it. I saw the dog doing the damage. Later, I went next door to complain. Defensively she denied that her dog had gotten out.

Just then her mother walked into view and said, "My daughter does not lie."

The two incidents above both really point out the same thing. Children become an extension of most people's ego. When we say something about children, it's almost as if we were saying something about the parent. When I said Lisa was pretty, her father beamed. In his thinking, I was really saying something about him. When I accused the neighbor girl of lying, her mother took that as a personal accusation.

Although it may never enter our minds to criticize our grandchildren, when we make an innocent suggestion about discipline to their parents it can often be interpreted as personal criticism. When our children want advice on how to raise their own children, they ask. Many of us grandparents are too quick to offer "suggestions" which are often veiled criticisms.

One psychologist said, "The first rule for grandparents is, shut up." He went on to say that we rarely make a mistake by keeping quiet about our grandchildren. We more likely make a mistake by voicing our opinion.

The second law then ought to be, never give advice to the parents of your grandchildren, on *anything*, unless we're asked.

It's easy for me to jump in and give my advice when I see my daughter frustrated over changing the baby's diaper, when she's nervously trying to feed him, when she's not giving him what I consider a nutritional diet or feeding at a proper time. I have to work at zipping my lip.

Many grandparents, seeing their children floundering helplessly in handling an infant or a young child, say to themselves, "They'll thank me for this good advice." Unfortunately, they won't. No matter how badly they're handling things, they tend to resent our advice unless they ask for it.

If we remind ourselves of this simple fact of ego extension, we understand that criticism of the child is criticism of the parent.

A better way of helping our grandchildren is to help their parents. We do this by complimenting them when they do things right, by encouraging them, by giving advice only when asked for.

God, help me not to be a know-it-all just because I'm a grandparent. Help me not to offer advice unless it's asked for. Amen.

Keep Growing

> Our life is cut short by your anger; it fades away like a whisper. Seventy years is all we have—eighty years, if we are strong; yet all they bring us is trouble and sorrow; life is soon over and we are gone.
>
> Psalms 90:9, 10 TEV

Week 3, Day 2

"All I want to do is relax, go fishing once a week, and enjoy my grandchildren," Clyde said to me once. And that's all he wanted!

I've often thought that it was unfortunate. He was sixty-seven years old, his health was still good; yet he had stopped growing. He took an attitude very much like that in Psalm 90. Most of us have about seventy or eighty years. Life is full of all kinds of troubles and sorrows, then it's over and we're gone. It's what we do with our life that makes the difference.

Being a grandparent doesn't mean we're through with life or that we cannot continue enriching ourselves. Being a grandparent is a different stage of life, but it is not the end of life.

Being a grandparent can be a wonderful opportunity to do new things in life. Now that our children are all gone from home, my wife is doing some of the things that she didn't have opportunities to do before. She not only works, but she's been going to school part-time.

More and more colleges are enrolling older students, folks who now have the time and still have the health and energy to enrich themselves. Other older adults are going into volunteer programs, so that they can serve other people and continue to grow.

Age and having grandchildren never signals us to give up. When we become grandparents it usually means we're in a stage of life where we can begin to slow down a little. Life is no longer as hectic as it once was. We are probably fairly well established in our career or even retired. Money problems are not nearly as acute as they were during the child-bearing years. Age and wisdom have enabled us to mellow. We're able to see life from a more relaxed point of view.

We can enjoy life, and we can enjoy it by continuing to grow. As a grandparent I made a decision last year that every year I was going to take on a new project. It would be a project that would be mentally demanding of me and would require several months, maybe as long as a year. For this current year, I decided to work on my New Testament Greek. I was once quite proficient in reading my New Testament in the original language, but over the years I lost it. In January I found my Greek grammar and have been systematically going through the book, chapter by chapter. Just like a young student I'm memorizing verb stems and noun endings. I'm determined to keep my mind active and alert.

I know of one couple, both in their late fifties, who have discovered square dancing. Others are taking courses on cooking or cake decorating. I know one man who is studying law and plans to take the bar exam. Will he ever practice? At the moment that doesn't seem important to him. He's growing and learning new things, and continuing to widen his horizon.

Think what wonderful opportunities we have in this

day and in this country. We're grandparents, but we're still young enough to try new things. We don't have to just sit in a corner and wait to die. The choice is ours.

God, You created the universe and all of us. Not only do I want to enjoy life; I want to continue expanding my horizons. Help me to do that today—and every day. Amen.

Learning, Too

" '. . . Out of the mouth of babes and sucklings
thou hast brought perfect praise.' "

Matthew 21:16 RSV

Week 3, Day 3

When two-year-old Michael first began to talk, one of his first words was *boat*. Whenever he rode in the car with us and saw a boat in someone's backyard he pointed and shouted, "Boat, boat!"

Truck was another word, even though he didn't say it clearly. We discovered that whenever Michael was with us, we were constantly lookiong for boats and trucks to point them out to him, so he could repeat his newly learned words.

Michael practiced and learned. I also learned something from the experience. I found myself looking, really looking. Even though I was searching for boats and trucks I began to notice lawns, flowers, and trees. I'd start pointing them out to Michael. I'd say, "See the pretty tree." "Look at the beautiful cat." As I pointed out the beauties of life, I realized that I had done this because *he* had called my attention to the simple things of life.

We often think of ourselves as the great teachers. We have amassed great knowledge and learning and we can

pass it on to our children, and especially to our grandchildren. We can also learn.

Most of us became involved in our careers as our
children were growing up—especially we fathers. Many
of us lost the wonder of nature, the joy of seeing fresh
green leaves on the trees, smelling the flowers, or enjoying a sunrise. One of the benefits of being a grandparent
is that we rediscover these things with our children's offspring. As we point out beautiful views and marvelous
miracles of nature, they become fresh to us. We learn as
we teach.

Some of the great works of literature have been telling
us these truths all along. Remember Little Lord Faunt-
leroy who taught his crusty grandfather how to relax
and enjoy life? In *Silas Marner* the little child taught the
miser to enjoy life and the pleasure of generosity. The
lessons are always there; we're just not always open to
receive them.

Perhaps that's one reason the verse, "Out of the
mouths of babes and sucklings," has such a shock ap-
peal to us. We expect knowledge to come from mature
minds. Yet sometimes children, merely by pointing out
the obvious, or even helping us look again at the com-
monplace, teach us new things.

One grandmother told me that she was talking on the
phone to a friend who was quite a bore. In order to get
rid of her she finally said, "I've got to run; someone's
ringing the doorbell." As soon as she had hung up, she
looked and saw her granddaughter in front of her.

"Grandma, you told a lie."

That grandmother confessed to me, "I realized then as
I never had before that a white lie is still a lie. It took my
grandchild to make me aware of that truth. She shamed
me by her innocence and honesty."

Out of the mouths of babes and sucklings . . .

*God, even though I have reached the middle of my life and
know so much, help me always to be a learner. Help me
truly learn and relearn truths my grandchildren and other
youngsters can teach me. Amen.*

From Our Roots

> Listen, my people, to my teaching, and pay at-
> tention to what I say. I am going to use wise
> sayings and explain mysteries from the past,
> things we have heard and known, things that
> our fathers told us. We will not keep them
> from our children; we will tell the next genera-
> tion about the Lord's power and his great
> deeds and the wonderful things he has done.
>
> Psalms 78:1–4 TEV

Week 3, Day 4

When I was a child, an old man named Mr. Lee lived
with us for several years. He was like a grandfather to
me, and one of the things he did was to talk about the
past. I remember his telling me the first time he ever saw
an automobile and how it scared him. He also told me
about the first time he had ever seen electricity at work,
when he turned on a light. This was absolutely amazing
to him. How many things we take for granted today.

All of us are part of living history. We may not realize
it, but we are. The things that have happened in our life
may seem quite ordinary to us, but we as grandparents
have had experiences that our children and grandchildren can never have. I remember the first time I ever
saw television. I could hardly believe that something
was happening in one part of the United States and I
was a thousand miles away viewing it at the same time.

Even though I was young during World War II, I remember rationing and little red points for meat and the
problems of buying sugar, chocolate, and gum. I remember what it was like the first time I flew in a twin-engine
plane out of Chicago. During my military days I rode
halfway across the United States in a train. Those are ex-

periences my children and grandchildren will never know. The best they can know is if I share it with them.

In the last few years we've been reminded of our roots and origins. Many are now dedicated to tracing their heritage back as far as they can.

Yet some people hesitate to share their stories with their own children and grandchildren. Perhaps they feel the new generations won't be interested. Sometimes they aren't. But sometimes it's either because of the way the stories are told or because the same stories are told over and over. Too many parents tell stories about doing chores or trudging through miles of snowdrifts to get to school, and very little about being mischievous and having fun. No wonder kids are turned off.

Some parents are reluctant to talk about their childhood because they weren't happy times. Why does childhood always have to be happy? In fact, our children and grandchildren have their moments of great sadness and unhappiness too. When we share with them some of our unhappy experiences, it gives them a more realistic view of life. They begin to understand that life isn't always happy and that we have problems whether we're four years old or eighty-four.

One of the things we may need to remind ourselves of is that a small person in a world full of grown-ups constantly finds rules that don't make sense and children can be greatly frightened. Childhood can be a miserable time. As I look back on my own, I have highlights of good times and memorable experiences, but there are other times when I was quite miserable. Knowing that other people have experienced hard times, and that life is both hardship and delight, helps children as they learn to face life's problems. We don't need to moralize, but we can let our stories speak for themselves.

Because I'm a writer, I often use my own childhood as illustrations in my books. My hope is that as my grandchildren get older and read things I've written, they will not only understand me better, but they will also appreciate some of their own roots.

Whether you would choose to write down your experiences, put them on cassette tape, or simply tell them orally to your children, we have a great deal we can teach them from our own experiences. Consider writing down your story or putting it on tape. Our life stories can be inspiring to our children and grandchildren, but the incidents teach, too.

As I share with my children and grandchildren the way God has worked in my life, it helps them to understand that God is there in our times of need. They begin to grasp that being a Christian is an everyday job and that we can call upon God in our happy times as well as our times of problems. We teach our children and grandchildren a great deal simply by relating our own spiritual experiences.

After all, when we stop to think about the Bible, that's largely what the book is. It's a retelling of the great incidents in the faith-history of God's people. They had experiences with God. They wrote them down and passed them on from one generation to another. What better way to communicate our faith and our values to our children than by sharing and retelling our experiences!

God of all history, as I tell my story to my children and grandchildren, help me to remember that part of my faith comes from knowing the story of Your people. Amen.

The Gossip Flow

> Gossip is so tasty! How we love to swallow it!
>   Proverbs 26:22 TEV

Week 3, Day 5

"And you know what my mommy did?"

Sometimes it's better not to let the child give the answer to that question. If the child is merely reciting an incident that happened at home, that may be all right. However, I know grandparents who want every morsel of information about what goes on in their children's home. When the grandchildren come, they pump them.

This kind of a situation eventually causes conflict. Children are smart enough to know when they are being used. That encourages children to make more of a story than need be.

The Lillian Hellman play called *The Children's Hour* was first presented in 1934. The plot revolves around a manipulating little girl who, in answer to her grandmother's prying, makes up a story. She implies that the two single women who operate her boarding school are lesbian. This naturally horrifies the grandmother and the story unfolds around that child's lie, which includes the suicide of one of them. As much to be blamed as the lying child was the grandmother who prompted it.

When I used to teach school I occasionally said to parents who came to me with misquotes and misconceptions of things that were going on in my classroom, "If you promise to believe only fifty percent of what your children tell you about me, I promise to believe only fifty percent of what they tell me about you." That usually ended it.

However, gossip is very sweet to some people. They want all the details and they want to know everything they can. Yet people who encourage gossip usually get hurt. Resentment builds up, problems develop and usually over such a thing as "But Johnny said that you said . . . ."

It's better, when a child says something about his mother or father that can be taken as gossip or problematic, that we as grandparents stop the flow. We can simply say, "I really don't want to talk about that," or "It's possible you may have misunderstood. Let's talk about something else." If we encourage the children to gossip they will bring to us anything they hear—or imagine. And I've never seen a happy gossip!

God, gossipers usually only want to hear the bad. Keep my ears closed to those kinds of things. Let me hear only the good, the beautiful, and the helpful. May my mouth speak only the good, the beautiful, and the helpful. Amen.

A Welcome Place

As Jesus and his disciples went on their way,
he came to a village where a woman named
Martha welcomed him in her home. She had a
sister named Mary, who sat down at the feet of
the Lord and listened to his teaching.

Luke 10:38, 39 TEV

Week 3, Day 6

"This is your home, too," I can hear Mary say. "You're
always welcome—as if we had to tell you."

We have no record of any such conversation in the
Bible; yet several times the Gospels mention Jesus going
to the town of Bethany, which was not far from Jerusa-
lem. He stayed at the home of Mary, Martha, and Lazarus. When Lazarus died, He even brought him back to
life. It's the only home mentioned in the Gospels where
Jesus actually visited and stayed. It makes me assume
that that family held a special relationship to Jesus.

When I think of special relationships, that certainly
fits grandparents and grandchildren. Like most grandparents, we love having our grandchildren visit. Most of
us think of their visits as special times in our lives. We
look forward to their coming, whether it's only for dinner or to spend an afternoon, or perhaps coming for the
weekend.

I know grandparents who keep a guest room just for
their four grandchildren. They invite them to come one
at a time. When that one child comes, he or she is a very
special person in that house. They plan all meals around
that child's favorite foods. The grandparents arrange
recreation and other activities according to what the
child wants. No wonder those four grandchildren look

upon their grandparents' house as a very special place to visit.

As grandparents we can provide that kind of welcome atmosphere for our children's children. Whether we think our children are doing as adequate a job of parenting as we did doesn't matter. We have things to offer those children that only grandparents can share. For one thing, we usually can give them more time. We can talk to them in a more relaxed atmosphere. That very atmosphere makes their visits special times, and they feel as though it's a privilege to come. And because it's a privilege they look upon each occasion as special. Grandparents' homes represent special places for some children, a place of refuge from the others in the family, a change of pace from school and the hassles of a fast-paced world, an opportunity to relax.

Whatever the reason or occasion for grandchildren coming, we can always make it a welcome place for them.

God, help me always to be a sensitive grandparent, making my home a welcome place for my grandchildren. Amen.

A Different Life-style

> Parents, do not treat your children in such a way as to make them angry. Instead, raise them with Christian discipline and instruction.
>
> Ephesians 6:4 TEV

Week 3, Day 7

"There's so much noise over there I don't know how that baby ever sleeps."

"You'd think they'd never heard of disciplining children, bringing them up that way. Why, we always taught our children to say 'Yes, ma'am' and 'No, sir.' Those children are running around like they've never been taught anything."

"She's a good mother, but you ought to see the way they eat. They have meals whenever they want them and don't eat enough of the proper foods."

Those are almost exact quotes from grandparents. What they really have not understood is that our children have different life-styles than we do. We might not like their choices, but that's reality.

Every generation must make its own set of rules and accept its own code of values. We can try to force our values upon our children, and sometimes we're successful. But if we're good parents and do our best to train our children to be good people and to follow Jesus Christ, they can still be different and not necessarily wrong.

Who's to say that we're right and they're wrong? I remember when our first daughter was only a few months old. We kept music playing in our house quite a bit. One grandmother (not related to us) was horrified. "How can you expect that child to sleep?"

We patiently tried to explain to her that our daughter had gotten used to the noise and that people talking or music playing, the doorbell, honking cars, and barking dogs didn't disturb her.

I don't think we ever convinced that well-intentioned grandmother. Every time she came to our house during those first few months, she tiptoed in and whispered. More than once she would admonish me to lower my voice. I conformed rather than offend her.

She had the affliction of many grandparents. Because I do something a certain way and believe it's the best method, that makes it right. If you do it differently, that makes you wrong.

When we raise our children and send them out on their own, we release them. Releasing our children means that basically our work is done. We're there if they need us, there to offer advice if asked for. But they must establish their own life-style. Part of *our* maturing as grandparents is to recognize that difference and appreciate it for what it is—*merely a difference.*

All-wise God, give me the wisdom to accept differing life-styles for my children and their children. Help me accept them and love them just as they are. Amen.

Making a Visit

> "If one of you is planning to build a tower, he sits down first and figures out what it will cost, to see if he has enough money to finish the job."
>
> Luke 14:28 TEV

Week 4, Day 1

"I love my mother," Julie said, "and it's always nice when we go to visit her. But by the end of the second day I'm about ready to turn around and come home."

When our grandchildren live a long distance from us, anticipating their visit is wonderful. Sometimes anticipation of the visit is more pleasant than the visit itself! By the time we get to the farewell kisses, our feelings are a mixture of love and of relief at finally saying good-bye. At the same time we feel guilty for feeling so good about saying good-bye. We want to avoid these kinds of visits.

Many problems could be avoided if grandparents and parents took more time in preparation. Sometimes family members don't bother to do anything special for one another because they think they're family, not company, and "they won't mind."

Unfortunately, this isn't always so. Family members do mind if the house isn't clean, bathroom towels aren't hung, and meals not on time. Slipshod households tell others we're not looking forward to their visit and have done nothing to make it better. We've set everything against the visit before it happens.

The first thing I suggest when we are expecting our grandchildren to visit is to plan for them. Plan as if they are special (which they are) and we want the house in perfect order. Prepare gourmet meals. At least we want to take special care to do everything we can to make this a significant event in the lives not only of our children but of our grandchildren as well.

When we're visiting, let's try to be good guests. Let's try not to be hypocritical if things aren't the way we hoped they would be. I suggest also that we plan our arrival and our stay so that they cause a minimal amount of disruption to the household. Our children and grandchildren have their own lives quite apart from us. No matter how much they love us, our coming is a disruption.

Let's also try not to visit our grandchildren when the other set of grandparents are there unless none of us are staying in the house. Two sets of grandparents can cause trouble. It can also be an overwhelming amount of company for both our children and grandchildren. As I point out elsewhere, there's always the tendency to engage in competition for the grandchildren's affections and create a situation that smart children learn to exploit.

If we have a choice, let's plan our arrival so that no one will have to leave work or other duties in the middle of the day to pick us up. One way is to think of our children as friends we are going to visit and treat them as considerately as we would a close friend.

As for the length of our visit, it's better to have it too short than too long. A friend of mine says, "Visitors are like fish. After the third day they smell." It's far better for everyone to feel, "I wish it could have lasted longer," than to say, "Thank goodness it's over."

Visiting our grandchildren or having them visit us can be a wonderful time, but it takes planning. We need to think of what it's going to cost us in time and money. We also need to think about the emotional and the physical toll.

By planning ahead, we can minimize the negative elements.

Lord God, help me consider the cost to us and to our children and grandchildren before we make plans to visit. When we visit one another, help us to make the most of these times together. May they be truly enjoyable for all of us. Amen

Long-Distance Grandparents

Finally hearing good news from a distant land
is like a drink of cold water when you are dry
and thirsty.

Proverbs 25:25 TEV

Week 4, Day 2

Shirley and I have been fortunate. Our children live fairly close to us and so we're able to see our grandchildren regularly. Unfortunately, all grandparents aren't so lucky.

The closest I've ever been to this is when our own children were quite young. We served as missionaries in a foreign country and our children had to go away to boarding school. We saw them every three months.

My wife often said the hardest thing about being a missionary was being separated from our children. At the same time she said one of the most joyful things about being a missionary is getting a letter from your children or enjoying them when they came home.

Some of us are the occasional or long-distance grandparents. Our children and grandchildren live far away from us and we miss much of their growing stages. For many of us it's hard to think of our grandchildren growing up without knowing us and without having our influence. We can't always bridge the distance, but there are things we can do.

For instance, children get few letters whether they are four or fourteen. We can write to them. We can send postcards and nice letters. I heard of one husband-and-wife team who write a grandparent newspaper. Once a month they make a kind of newspaper-looking sheet of paper with all kinds of information which is both accurate and informative, and send it to their own grandchildren. It contains items such as a cat being lost in the neighborhood or a trip to the mountains.

In recent years the telephone company has boasted how cheap it is to call long-distance. Young children get an opportunity to talk on the telephone. They love it. At my daughter's home when the telephone rings, seven-year-old Danny runs completely through the house just to answer.

Tape cassettes can add another dimension to long-distance communications. Tapes have advantages. They are more personal than a written letter. Our grandchildren can play them as many times as they wish. Younger children especially can understand a cassette letter more easily than a written one. The children can also return our communications by making cassettes of their own.

Another thing that we can do is visit our grandchildren or even have them visit us. Nowadays it's possible to travel great distances by plane and in very short periods of time. Children can fly alone and airlines cooperate beautifully in making sure that the children get on and off planes. There are all kinds of ways that we can bridge the distance.

Of course, if our children and grandchildren are living away from us, it's never the same as if they lived on the other side of town. There will always be that long distance. But being able to communicate with them through sending of postcards or cassettes makes them seem a little closer.

We realize our need to be close to our grandchildren,

but we're also helping the children by reminding them that they have roots and that there's somebody named Grandma and Grandpa loving them. They may not always be able to remember what we look like or our favorite colors, but they know we're there because we remind them. Good news from us may be just as meaningful to them as it is for us to hear from our grandchildren.

O God, when my grandchildren are separated from me, help them not to forget me and help me to remember them also. I'm reminded that You never forget us and that You're never far away. I thank You for this. Amen.

Competing

How wonderful it is, how pleasant, for God's
people to live together in harmony!

Psalms 133:1 TEV

Week 4, Day 3

Jane and Rich came to my office and together we planned their wedding. After that it got complicated. Jane's mother had all sorts of plans. Rich's parents tried to tell them how the wedding ought to be. The two prospective in-laws grew so angry with each other that they would call each other on the phone and argue. Finally Jane and Rich came to the church, and the three of us had a private wedding ceremony.

"This is the only way we can do it," Rich said, "without hurting one side of the family."

"No matter what we do, somebody's going to be offended," Jane said, "so we decided we might as well offend everybody equally."

The couple now have two children. The situation has gotten no better between the parents of the couple. They still don't like each other. But more than that, their trouble really stems from competing—they compete for the affection and time of their offspring.

For instance, Jane's mother said, "Of course we always are together on Christmas Day. That's our family's tradition."

To which Rich's father said, "We always have Christmas dinner at two o'clock. I expect you to be here as well as the other children and grandchildren."

Sometimes we grandparents make it very difficult on our children. We force them into choices they don't want to make. Rich and Jane have considered moving to another state. Had it not been that Rich has great business opportunities in this area, he would have moved right after their marriage. Every year the situation continues to be a problem. When birthdays come along, and especially during the Thanksgiving and Christmas holidays, the battles rage.

Not just holiday periods, but the grandparents compete in the giving of gifts. One set of grandparents gives toys to the children. The other set tries to get something better. The competition between the two sets of grandparents is a continual sense of disturbance. Rich and Jane have decided to avoid both sets of parents.

As a pastor, I frequently see this happen—even if not so openly. So when our children married we said to each of them, "When it comes to birthdays and holidays, we have our own family tradition. We plan to keep it. You are welcome and we hope you will come. But we don't demand that you come, and we will not compete with the other set of parents."

As preparation for the time of their marriage and separate families, when our children reached their early teens we changed our Christmas celebration. We now do everything on Christmas Eve. That means that on Christmas Day they are free to do anything or go anywhere they wish. Over the years it has worked out beautifully, and we've never had difficulty with the other grandparents.

Last Thanksgiving none of our children came to visit us. They had other plans. We love our children and grandchildren and know they love us. We're secure. Because we're secure in our relationship, we don't need to compete. We can work toward making the lives of our children and grandchildren more harmonious and pleasant.

God, teach me not to resent or to compete with the other grandparents. Help me to accept other grandparents, and as much as possible to live in harmony with our children and grandchildren. Amen.

$

Truth, wisdom, learning, and good sense—these are worth paying for, but too valuable for you to sell.

Proverbs 23:23 TEV

Week 4, Day 4

"I know you just can't afford it, so let me pay."

I actually heard a grandmother say this to her son-in-law in a public restaurant. I could tell by the look on his face that he was embarrassed. Perhaps he felt like a charity case.

Many of us grandparents—by the time we reach that stage in life—are fairly secure financially. At least, we're better off than our children who are just starting families. One of the best ways I know to destroy relationships is by unwise "buying" for our children.

Is it all right to give them an occasional check to help on groceries? Of course, this depends to some extent upon the family's financial situation—and our own. If my children are struggling to make ends meet and we're well off, we can help. But we also need to do it diplomatically.

When we realize that our children are under a financial

burden, we can send them a check or give them some help; but *don't mention it again*.

I know one grandfather who is very well off, provides adequately for his grandchildren by constantly buying them clothes and toys, which the parents appreciate. What they don't appreciate is his constant reminders of the money he spends on them. Granted that the grandparent may be generous, but he does not help the relationship by his constant references to giving.

Sometimes we suspect a financial need and we can offer help. If it's refused, then drop the subject.

If you are a traditional grandmother who believes that when a man is present he's the one who should pay the check, this could present problems. Of course if your own husband is around that's no real problem. But what if he's not? Customs have changed, and today it's not necessary for the man to pay. But if it makes you feel more comfortable and you want to pay, why not slip your son or son-in-law the money? It's preferable to do this before you go out to eat rather than in the restaurant itself.

The main advice that I offer on handling money with our children and grandchildren is to do it lovingly and discreetly. We don't want them to learn to depend on us. When our children marry, they cut themselves off from us so that they become independent beings. If we are constantly there to pick up pieces, to pay their bills, we teach them to depend on us. In the long run that's destructive.

If we really love our children we will help when it's needed or when we're asked. But we'll also encourage them to be financially and emotionally independent.

Lord God, help me to be sensitive to the money needs of my children. Help me not to be too quick to help nor too slow. Lead me by Your Spirit as I try to be the most loving grandparent I know how to be. Amen.

Giving Gifts

"Please, sir, accept this present I have brought
you, and give it to your men."

1 Samuel 25:27 TEV

Week 4, Day 5

My wife's mother was the kind of grandmother every
child ought to have. Every once in a while she would
surprise our children with a gift, and usually not an expensive one—occasionally clothes, or a book, maybe a
game. I never saw her gifts fail to interest our children.
Mom Brackett was a teacher of elementary children and
understood children. She also sensed the kinds of things
that our children enjoyed.

For instance, when our older daughter was five she
took her out and had her hair washed and curled. What
I didn't know is that my daughter had passed by beauty
shops and had asked several times what it was like and
wanted to have her hair done. It was a great experience
when she came home smiling and laughing with her
curly top.

As grandparents we have the opportunity to offer
these kinds of gifts. There are some warnings we need to
be aware of however. One of them is *appropriateness*.

Another is to be sure that our generosity causes no
problems within the family. Some parents are sensitive
about their children receiving gifts—even from grandparents. It's always a good idea to make sure it's not
going to cause any difficulty. For instance, we did not
like our children to have candy; yet we had relatives
who constantly bombarded our children with every kind
of mint, bubble gum, and candy bars. It was difficult to
explain to them that we limited the amount of sweets
our children ate.

The best kind of gift has no strings attached. We don't need to buy children's love. Some people try to give gifts instead of themselves. I remember a boy who received expensive gifts from an uncle, yet he seemed to have very little use for them. I never asked him directly, but his mother said to me, "His uncle sends him gifts, but he doesn't think his uncle really loves him."

When we give a gift of money for a birthday, the child makes his/her own decision what to do with it. That child may use the money foolishly, but that's none of our business. We give them money as an expression of love. What the child does with the gift is his/her own business.

Someone said, "Gifts are both an extension of the giver and an evaluation of the recipient." Some people give gifts because they feel guilty about not giving time or attention. Others want to appear more generous or wealthy than they are. Some people give small gifts because they don't want to appear ostentatious. Or they may communicate a message: a person receiving the gift is getting just what he/she deserves—very little.

In the Bible, a woman named Abigail had an oafish husband who threatened David, and she feared for her husband's life. She got a cartload of food and took it to David as a gift. Abigail recognized that David was going to be the next king. She also knew that poachers had been around. Yet David and his men had kept their cattle from harm. She gave her gift with no strings attached.

That's the best kind of gift. When we give freely and generously from our hearts we don't buy love—we don't have to. Gifts don't buy love from anyone; they can only buy attention, and temporary attention at that. Gifts given from a caring heart and given simply because you want to please the recipient are the best gifts of all. That's how God operates. He gave us Jesus, His best gift.

Generous God, help me to be both generous and wise in giving to my grandchildren. Amen.

Receiving Gifts

Be thankful in all circumstances. This is what
God wants from you in your life in union with
Christ Jesus.

1 Thessalonians 5:18 TEV

Week 4, Day 6

"I get so much junk," one grandmother lamented.
"Every Friday and Saturday my three grandchildren
come to visit. They bring me pictures and objects
they've made. I don't know what to do with it all, and
I'm getting tired of receiving it."

I feel sorry for that grandmother. I think she misunderstood. She didn't know how to receive gifts and be
thankful for them. I know that woman fairly well. She
doesn't receive any kind of gift easily.

As grandparents, we often receive gifts from our
grandchildren. They may not always know how to give
appropriate gifts. We can teach them a great deal about
the giving and receiving by *our* attitudes when they give
us gifts.

When our grandchildren are preschoolers, they will
do things such as try to draw pictures and say, "This is
Grandma and Grandpa. This is your house." When they
get into grade school, they not only draw pictures but
sometimes make their handprints in plaster or a variety
of objects that have more sentimental than artistic value.

But what do we do with all these things? Particularly
how do we receive them when we have a limited amount
of space? We may not want to display our grandchildren's art over our living-room couch no matter how
much we love the artist. Most grandchildren don't ex-

pect us to do that. They are giving us a gift—which is giving of themselves—it's the giving and the receiving that is more important to them than the displaying.

One creative grandfather always photographs gifts or works of art and then puts the print in a photo album. He has quite a collection now. His grandchildren are in their teens, and occasionally they'll get out the photo album and say things like, "Did I really make that for you, Grandpa?" It's a lovely memory book for both the grandchildren and the grandparents.

How about using the refrigerator door as a revolving art gallery? Most things can be held up with magnets, shown for a limited period, then replaced. This becomes an especially nice way to do things when we have several grandchildren who visit frequently or when we have budding artists who are especially productive.

Whether or not we display the *objets d'art*, keep at least some of them. You can store them in a closet or perhaps in a box that slides under the bed. Preserving those works of love will be worth the trouble it takes to find a place to put them. I don't think children are flattered so much at the time. Later when they find out that we've held onto these things for many years, they're touched.

When my wife's mother died and we were going through her papers and possessions, we discovered letters and drawings that she had kept. I thought it was a very loving and sentimental thing to do.

Above all, let's be enthusiastic about receiving our grandchildren's gifts. After all, they went to the time and trouble to make them and they made them for us. It doesn't matter whether Mother or Dad or teacher suggested them; the point is, they made them. It's their work. Generally, nobody forced them to choose us as the recipients. They give us gifts solely because they want to.

We can have another object lesson out of this. Not only do we show them enthusiastically that we appreciate their gifts, but we can send little thank-you notes through the mail even if they live next door. That's a good way to train our grandchildren to thank people for their gifts. We set examples ourselves.

We all like gifts. We need to realize that the thought and the love behind the gift exceeds the value of the object we receive. When a child offers us a picture or a carving, no matter how badly done, that child is offering himself or herself to us. In the admonition of the Apostle Paul, let's be thankful at all times.

Father God, teach me to always be thankful for every gift. And in every opportunity help me show people that I appreciate their kindness and their gifts. Help me most of all to be thankful for Your gift of life through Jesus Christ. Amen.

Gapping the Generations

> What you have done will be praised from one generation to the next; they will proclaim your mighty acts.
>
> Psalms 145:4 TEV

Week 4, Day 7

A man approximately my age sat next to me on the plane. Earlier he had told me about his three grandchildren. Later he said, "I don't know what's happened to this generation. All they think about is drugs, sex, and violence."

While he didn't say it, he implied that this generation is the worst one that's ever come along. I didn't respond to him because I don't think he wanted to hear what I had to say.

As I sat listening, I remembered my own father's words. I was sixteen and listening to a Frank Sinatra song on the radio. My father lectured me on the filthy words that Sinatra was singing. I heard nothing wrong with the lyrics. I thought at the time that when I grew up I would never tell my children how awful they were or how terrible the world had become.

Somehow each generation thinks the one following it is worse than their own. We're constantly talking about the decline of morals and trying to relive the good old days. I know people older than I who grew up in the depression years. To hear them tell it you would think that was a time of great peace and serenity. I came at the end of the depression but knew enough and remember my parents telling how awful it was. Life wasn't so wonderful in the good old days.

We grandparents need to remind ourselves that each generation is *different*. That doesn't mean better or worse, only different. For one thing, children are much more sophisticated today. The media, especially TV, have a lot to do with this. There was a time when we could convince children that they needed to be moral and upright in order to succeed. Today we can't use those kinds of arguments. The TV screen informs us of illegal activities in high positions, as well as corruption by corporation executives and politicians. Our television-era children are aware of the entire world far more than we were. They know names of places like Afghanistan and El Salvador long before the age we ever thought about them.

Someone jokingly said, "If Booth Tarkington wrote his novel *Seventeen* today he'd have to call it *Twelve.*"

One generation comes along and the next one moves out of its way. We can move on joyfully, or we can go out screaming and cursing the changes. Then our children, and especially our grandchildren, can look down upon us as old-fashioned people who just don't adjust to this new world.

If we really want to bridge the generation gap, the first thing we need to do is to come to terms with the fact that while our grandchildren may be different, their generation is neither better nor worse. We can instill sound moral values in our grandchildren. We teach them more by the way we enjoy life than by pointing our fingers at those who live wrongly.

Frankly, I think our children are living in the greatest period in the history of the world. They've enjoyed more scientific advances than any other generation.

I'm excited to be part of this world and to see my children enjoy a more meaningful life. Diseases that snuffed out the life of my childhood friends will not attack my grandchildren. Recently I learned that smallpox has now been eliminated in the world. Next perhaps polio. One day even cancer. Each generation is making is own strides in progress. The generation of our grandchildren always differs from our own. We can help bridge that gap by accepting them as they are.

God, help me bridge the generation gap by accepting my children's children as they are and sharing with them Your wonderful love, rather than criticizing them and being negative about life. Amen.

Are You Talking to Me?

A young man named Eutychus was sitting in
the window, and as Paul kept on talking, Eutychus got sleepier and sleepier, until he finally
went sound asleep and fell from the third story
to the ground. When they picked him up, he
was dead. But Paul went down and threw
himself on him and hugged him. "Don't
worry," he said, "he is still alive!" ... They
took the young man home alive and were
greatly comforted.

Acts 20:9–12 TEV

Week 5, Day 1

The Apostle Paul was preaching in Ephesus. He
preached a long time. And while this was going on, a
young man named Eutychus got sleepy and finally fell
asleep. Then he fell three stories out a window. Apparently a miracle was performed, and Eutychus was
taken home alive and well.

As I was reading the story of Eutychus recently, it
occurred to me that he probably didn't understand all
that Paul preached. Paul was talking primarily to adults
and he was a young man. Many times we adults (even
grandparents!) talk to our children as though they were
adults and understand everything.

We grandparents often need to learn to talk to children. We say the words, but we may not be talking in a
language they readily understand.

Because we're older and generally much larger physi-
cally, we not only look down when we talk to our children; we tend to talk down. Often adults talk to children
as though it's a one-way directive from adult to child.

They seldom listen—really listen—to the child's response. Sometimes two different messages are going on. A child tries to say one thing, and an adult is saying something quite different.

If we want children to listen, we have to learn to speak a language they understand. That means more than just avoiding large words or complicated explanations. It means first of all, simply *listening*—listening carefully to what the child says.

We also need to make sure they have understood what we've said. One way to find out is to simply ask, "Do you understand what I mean?"

A second thing we could do in talking to children is to hear what they say and put their feelings into words for them. For instance, children often use exaggerated statements. I heard a child the other day saying he wanted to die.

I knew the boy well enough to realize that wasn't what he meant. He felt quite unhappy and rejected.

I said to him, "You think the other children don't know how you feel? Is that right?" He replied by nodding his head yes. Pretty soon he talked to me and explained his sense of rejection by the group. Yet to say he wanted to die was his only way of explaining how miserable he felt.

At that time I heard the child and responded to him and tried to feed back the words he had given me. That is, I worked at seeing the situation from his viewpoint instead of only from my adult perspective. We adults often forget. We think because we say words, children understand. Or we take their words literally and assume we've understood. Talking to grandchildren involves not only patience, but working at hearing what they have to say and being careful that they understand us.

God, teach me to talk to my grandchildren so they really hear me. At the same time, help me to listen to them and understand what they're trying to say in the same way You always listen to me and understand. Amen.

Listen Up!

"If you have ears, then, listen to what the
Spirit says to the churches!"

Revelation 2:7 TEV

Week 5, Day 2

"I'll bet you like staying with your granddaddy, don't
you?" I asked the eight-year-old boy.

"Yeah, I guess," he said. "But I'm tired of him telling
me all the time everything he did when he was a boy."

Billy didn't go into detail, but I know the kind of thing
he was talking about. Those of us who are grandparents
have had many experiences. We've learned a lot of
things through our years of living. One danger for us is
that we want to tell everything we've learned.

If we've really learned during our years of living, one
of the best lessons is that of listening rather than talking.
The temptation, however, is to talk and to keep on talking, especially when we see our children handling their
children poorly or improperly, when we see our grandchildren making mistakes, when we know easier, faster,
or simpler ways of doing things.

Being grandparents also carries a lot of privileges.
One of them is *not* being a know-it-all. We have to overcome the temptation to hand out advice when it's not
needed, correcting problems that others may not know
exist, or giving advice "for your own good."

Not that this applies only to grandparents, but we
seem to have a higher dosage of the affliction. Perhaps
one reason is, we made a lot of the same mistakes ourselves. If our memories are really good, we may recall
that our parents and grandparents tried to offer us ad-

vice when it wasn't asked for, and we resented or rejected it.

Most of us need to be reminded about listening. Even in the Bible, the Apostle John writes to seven churches in the first three chapters of Revelation. He concludes each message with an exhortation to "Listen up." He would not have needed to write that if he knew that they easily heard what he had to say to them.

Just the other day someone reminded me of the old saying, "God gave us two ears and one mouth—that means we need to listen twice as much as we talk." That is still good advice for all of us, especially grandparents.

Lord God, help me listen up and to be slow to offer advice, especially when it's not asked for. Teach me to be a better listener than a better speaker. Amen.

Giving Advice

> . . . the time for silence and the time for talk.
>
> Ecclesiastes 3:7 TEV

Week 5, Day 3

Here is the best word about giving advice: don't.

Parents find themselves overwhelmed with advice. When it comes to babies, everyone is an expert. Everyone either has had a baby or has been one. Neighbors, doctors and nurses, friends, relatives—all tell the uncertain new mother and the intimidated new father what to do.

When our children were young I used to say, "The best experts on child care are childless couples and grandparents." I simply meant that both grandparents and childless couples constantly handed us advice and information.

It's natural that we grandparents have definite ideas on how to raise babies. However, we need to remind ourselves that new parents often lack assurance. Like anyone at a new job, they can be very touchy about criticism. As new parents gain confidence, that phase begins to pass. When they feel the need for advice and able to receive it, they can ask. In the meantime one of the best things we can do as grandparents is to let our children know that we'll be glad to tell them anything we can—anything they want to know that we know. But until they ask, we'll hold our tongue.

That's not easy, especially when we see Mom or Dad doing something that we feel is awkward or could be done in a different way. The advice still holds—don't offer it. Only if the parents ask should we offer help.

Some of the worst things we can say are words like, "if she were my child . . ." "I was wondering if you'd get around to noticing . . ." "I hate to criticize dear, but. . . ."

Because we're grandparents we are experts. We've raised our own children. We also did a pretty good job—not perfect, but pretty good. We had years of living that our children don't have. We can look ahead and often see the outcome of decisions that they may not be aware of. Yet they may not want to hear us.

One of the kindest things we can do for our children is to keep silent and to accept them without constantly trying to tell them a better way to handle things.

There's a time to speak and a time to keep silent. For most of us grandparents, it's the silence we still need to learn.

All-hearing God, help me to keep silent when my advice is not needed. Help me to be supportive, loving, and available when I am needed. Amen.

Discipline

Teach a child how he should live, and he will
remember it all his life.

Proverbs 22:6 TEV

Week 5, Day 4

"Chuck, if you touch that TV knob I'm going to slap
your hand."

"Don't you dare get into that refrigerator!"

"Tim, put that toy down this instant or I'm going to
spank you. Understand?"

These are typical of how parents and grandparents try
to guide the behavior of children. We threaten, scold or
yell. We give little lectures, we spank, we take away
privileges. Unfortunately, many of the methods we use
are ineffective. We're trying to teach children so that
they don't do undesirable things. We want to change
their behavior and their attitude. We do it several different ways.

I'm convinced that threatening and eventually pun-
ishing can be a disastrous way to teach our children. A
better way is positive reinforcement.

Positive reinforcement means simply rewarding children when they do something right. Every time Tommy
picks up his toys he receives a reward for it. That reward
may be a kiss or a hug. Granddad may simply say, "I
like the way you picked up your toys." The reward
could simply be someone saying, "I love you."

Our children learn as much from our attitude and our
behavior as they do from the words we speak. I've en-
countered many people who, long past the childhood
stages of life, are afraid of God. They only know about a

God who threatens and who punishes. Part of that they learned from childhood teachings. When they were bad they were punished and sometimes quite severely. They constantly feared being caught when they did something wrong. When they got to church they heard the thundering words of wrath that would one day come from God.

When we who are the grandparents have the opportunity to discipline our children, we can teach them much about behavior, about life, and even about the love of God simply by the way we discipline them.

Some have said that positive reinforcement really isn't discipline, but bribing. Call it what you will, we are simply saying that when we give children positive rewards for picking up toys, making their beds, reading books, hanging up their clothes, we are developing in them desirable habits that will carry them on to adult life.

For example, I remember when I was in the fifth grade. We were practicing penmanship and we were working on our capital letters. I made a capital *D*. The teacher passed my desk, looked down, and said, "That's very, very good" and moved on.

Until that time my penmanship had not been particularly good and I had not cared whether it was beautiful or not. But she recognized that I had put effort into it. I worked very hard the rest of that day on my penmanship and from then on. Two or three more times during the year my teacher commented on how well I was progressing. She didn't bribe me; she did encourage me.

We want to train our children. We train them by enforcing the positive and the good. When we love them and show them loving ways, we really are teaching them a lot about God. We're showing by example a God who loves us, rewards us, and does things for us simply because He loves us.

God, help me in the disciplining of my grandchildren to do it lovingly and to teach them about the positive side of life. Especially help me to let them know about the positive God who loves them. Amen.

Making Mistakes

Love is patient and kind ... love is not ill-
mannered or selfish or irritable. ...

                    1 Corinthians 13:4, 5 TEV

Week 5, Day 5

"Let her cry," Grandma says. "It won't hurt her."

"But I don't like my daughter to cry," the young
mother responds.

Who's right? That's not even the issue.

Perhaps the daughter *is* making a mistake. We know,
for instance, that crying does not injure children. It's
good for developing their lungs and is part of their
growing-up process. The young mother may make a
mistake running to her child too quickly.

But Grandma makes a mistake, too. She's telling her
daughter how to raise that child. As grandparents we
need to remind ourselves that all new parents are ama-
teurs. They also make mistakes.

As I think back, I sometimes resented my parents telling me how to raise our children. My mother and father
thought we were too strict. Shirley's mother implied that
she thought we were too lenient. We probably made
mistakes, but they were our mistakes.

Being a good grandparent means accepting the fact
that our children are going to live their own life-style
and they're going to make their own mistakes, just as we
did.

Learning to raise children is like learning other skills.
I remember when I learned to bowl. I developed into a
pretty fair bowler, but I made thousands of mistakes in
the process. I had to learn the footwork, how to hold the
ball, how to avoid lofting, and dozens of other things. I

didn't become a good bowler in a matter of weeks. It took me years. I also discovered that every time I bowled I could learn something new.

Our grown children had the right to learn how to be parents themselves by making thousands of mistakes. If we love them, we can allow them to make mistakes. We can see what they're doing and keep quiet or offer advice only when asked for.

Methods of child training have changed greatly in the past thirty years. Generally speaking there is a much more permissive attitude toward raising children. For one thing, our generation seemed obsessed with toilet training. Mothers prided themselves on training their infants before they were a year old or certainly by a year and a half. Today it's not uncommon to see three-year-olds running around in diapers. Is it right? Is it wrong? Who can say?

Good grandparents allow their children to raise their own children, trusting them in the same way that our parents trusted us. If we love our children and have taught them, we know that our own grandchildren are going to come out all right.

Loving grandparents allow their children to make mistakes just as other parents from the time of Adam and Eve have made mistakes.

God, help me allow my children to make mistakes in raising our grandchildren. Help our love be so strong and consistent that we'll overlook the things that we may consider wrong. Amen.

Handling Conflicts

> Get rid of all bitterness, passion, and anger.
> No more shouting or insults, no more hateful
> feelings of any sort. Instead, be kind and
> tender-hearted to one another, and forgive one
> another, as God has forgiven you through
> Christ.
>
> Ephesians 4:31, 32 TEV

Week 5, Day 6

"We had to cancel our bridge game, you know,"
Grandfather said.

"So next time give us a day's notice and we'll be glad
to babysit," Grandmother said.

That begins the conflict. Not that the grandparents
didn't want to take care of the children. They enjoy
spending an evening with the two little ones. They simply did not like the way the children were dumped on
them without warning. "We're being taken advantage
of," the grandfather said.

That's one area of conflict. Other conflicts arise no
matter how good the relationship between parents and
their children. We as grandparents will probably not be
immune from them. We need to learn to face the conflict
and to handle it creatively.

In the above example, the grandparents said, "If
you'll just simply call us a day ahead of time, we'll be
glad to keep the children." A more creative way might
be, "It bothers me when you bring the children by for us
to babysit without checking first to find out our plans."

Telling the children how we feel is better than order-
ing them to do something. Yet the message comes out
just as clear. What's wrong with our feeling joy, love,
anger, pain, hurt? Being upset happens to us all. How

we handle conflicts and what we do about them makes the difference. Usually we can tell someone how we *feel* and not put that person on the defensive. Unfortunately, many of us go from telling people how we feel to telling them what to do about it. We need to refrain from saying, "Dear, please call me next time first."

That last quote sounds fairly harmless, but it's almost guaranteed to make our daughter or son feel defensive (consciously or unconsciously). Whenever we tell someone what to do, that person feels attacked. Being attacked brings conflict whatever our intentions.

One way we, as grandparents, can learn to avoid conflict with our children (especially when it comes to grandchildren) is to relate our feelings. We leave it up to them as to how they react to the situation. If we tell them that it interferes with our plans or becomes an inconvenience when they drop in without warning and leave the children, we have not told them what to do, we have told them how we feel. That does not put them on the defensive. That means that now they have to make a decision.

The principle of telling other people how we feel, not telling them what to do about it, is a basic rule for good human relationships. It's an excellent principle for us to teach our grandchildren when they're old enough to absorb it. But in order to teach it to our grandchildren, we first have to learn to use it effectively ourselves. When we use the technique of telling people how we feel and not telling them what to do, we find that it helps avoid conflict or even straightens out conflict. Our children are human; they have feelings, too. Sometimes they are thoughtless or careless, but then so are we.

Because we love our children and grandchildren and they love us, we can learn to overcome conflicts and forgive each other's mistakes. After all, God is our father. He forgives our failures.

God, help us avoid conflicts with our children and grandchildren. Help us as much as possible to live together harmoniously and lovingly. Amen.

Sibling Rivalry

Love is patient and kind; it is not jealous or
conceited or proud.

1 Corinthians 13:4 TEV

Week 5, Day 7

"Your mother gave Fred a watch for graduation, but
she only gave a book for Jimmy's," the husband said to
his wife. He was simply saying that his child did not get
as much for a graduation present as the son's cousin. He
implied that the grandparents had been partial.

"My parents are always taking my sister's son camp-
ing, but they leave my kids at home. They've got plenty
of room in their camper, and our kids would love to go,
too."

These are the kinds of things that grandparents constantly have to watch. We call it sibling rivalry. Sibling
rivalry doesn't stop at the parental level; it's also charac-
teristic of grandparents. Grandparents on the father's
side often compete with those on the mother's side for
the love of their shared grandchildren. For instance, the
two sets of grandparents try to outdo each other with the
gifts they give at Christmas time or for birthdays. They
behave like two opposing teams, each trying to outscore
the other, rather than like two families trying to work together for the good of the children and the grandchildren.

Rivalry is based on the fact that each one of us wants
to have 100 percent of the love and affection of another
individual. Deep down your granddaughter may wish
her brother would vanish so she could have her parents
all to herself, or even have you exclusively as grandparents. When her brother disrupts games or makes fun of

his sister, he may be saying in a disguised form, "Get out of here and let me have Mom and Dad all to myself, or my grandparents all to myself."

Parents never really eliminate children's rivalry. The only way to dispose of the problem would be to get rid of all the children but one. The problem of sibling rivalry can be diminished, not eliminated. Sibling rivalry generally exists on an unconscious level. That means that when two sets of grandparents compete with each other, neither pair is aware of it. Parents and grandparents often do not realize they compete with one another for the love of the children.

Though parents and grandparents are grown adults, they sometimes act like eight-year-old children when they play the rivalry game. They correct the problem only as they become aware of it.

How do we become aware of rivalry? First we examine ourselves. Are we unconsciously trying to control or gain the upper hand of a grandchild?

For instance, although I never knew my grandmother Murphey, my two oldest sisters tell me that when they were fairly young they knew which of the two of them Grandmother Murphey preferred. Probably she had not specifically said so, but nonetheless she made it very clear that she really loved one and had little use for the other. Most grandparents aren't quite so blatant in their behavior, but children and grandchildren often feel any hint of inequality.

As grandparents we have to work hard when we have more than one child and particularly more than one grandchild, in order to be fair to all. It becomes quite important that we show that there is no difference in our attitude toward our offspring.

We need to recognize that our children and our grandchildren are different. They are different ages and in different stages of life. As grandparents, it's important to us that we try to eliminate any show of partiality among the children and grandchildren.

Sibling rivalry springs from jealousy, as when one child feels the other is loved more than she is. I remember when my daughters first entered their teens. There was a great deal of open rivalry between them. We, as their parents, thought we were treating both of them fairly. Yet each insisted that we loved the other more. This was a natural jealousy. This happens in almost all families. We probably cannot eliminate rivalry, but we can reduce it. We start resolving sibling rivalry when we stop kidding ourselves and admit that children, parents, even grandparents compete with one another. We all have jealous feelings. We are angered and hurt. That's part of being human. When rivalry and jealousy are under control, we can pay less attention to the role of rivals and concentrate on fulfilling roles as children, parents, and grandparents.

All-loving God, remind me that Your love is as great for me as it is for anyone else. In the same way, help me love my children and grandchildren equally. Amen.

The Blessing of Grandparenting

> Children are a gift from the Lord; they are a real blessing.
>
> Psalms 127:3 TEV

Week 6, Day 1

My wife, Shirley, was a good mother. She's an even better grandmother. I think this is true of many women. When they're raising their own children, they're quite emotionally involved, often high-strung, nervous. When the grandchildren come along, they relax more and enjoy the children because they're children.

A few months after our second grandson was born my wife said, "Being a grandparent means you can have a child without having to get pregnant." I knew what she meant, because my wife's pregnancies were always a difficult time. But it also meant that here was a new child to hold, to love, to influence, and to be around.

Being a grandparent offers other advantages. For instance, grandparents rarely have to change diapers. They seldom stay up all night with a sick child. They don't usually get stuck with running the child to the dentist or getting flu shots.

Grandparents have the best of two worlds. They can see their grandchildren part of the time, while the parents are stuck with the children all of the time.

When our children were small, I remember my mother used to remark, as I've heard others say since, "I'm always so glad when my grandchildren come and just as glad when they leave." She was saying that she looked forward to having them come, enjoyed their presence, but by the time they left, she was anxious for her privacy again.

Being a grandparent may mean you have a child of a different sex. I know one couple who raised three boys. They were excited when their sons married. They were even more excited when their first grandchild was a girl. Grandmother said, "At last I can buy pretty dresses for a little girl."

Being with children teaches us a lot about people who have children. Now that we're grandparents we can look objectively at the children we've raised, but even more at our grandchildren, because we did not give them birth and they're not with us all the time. We can better understand their problems and yet not be fully immersed in them.

I have a friend who is a grandfather, and yet he's a man who never really grew up. He enjoys having a good time and he said, "One of the nice things about being a grandfather is I can be silly with the children and I don't have to worry about being sophisticated."

Children come as a gift from God (Psalms 127:3). We enjoy this gift, now that we're grandparents, by watching our children's children mature. We do not have to put up with the disadvantages of parenthood, and yet we receive the blessings of the smiles, shared moments, and presence of our grandchildren on a limited basis. We have opportunities to cuddle, to teach, and to spend time with them. We've really got it made, haven't we?

God, thank You for the wonderful blessings that children bring. They truly are a gift from You. For this I thank You. Amen.

The Perfect Grandparent

> Everyone has sinned and is far away from God's saving presence.
>
> Romans 3:23 TEV

Week 6, Day 2

"I'm an absolute failure as a grandmother," she said. "I am so tied down with my job and other things that I don't fulfill all those wonderful plans I had when my grandchildren came along." She spoke to me out of deep remorse, convinced she had somehow failed.

Somehow Margaret had a vision of what a grandparent ought to be. She did not measure up to that vision. But then who of us ever lives up to all of our own expectations? There is no such thing as a perfect grandparent, a perfect parent, or even a perfect child. One of the things that the Bible makes clear is that all of us fail. We're sinners.

We fail. None of us live up to our own expectations.

What is a perfect grandmother anyway? Does it mean having to be always around when the children are there? Giving up our lives at their whim? Does being the perfect grandparent mean always having cookies on the table whenever the grandchildren pop in? Who can answer what the perfect grandparent ought to be?

Our problem is we have this inner sense that we don't live up to our own ideals. But then we never lived up to our own ideals as parents or even as children. We're not going to get any better as grandparents. How do we help ourselves? First by simply acknowledging that none of us is perfect and that all of us are tainted by the sinfulness that's common to humanity. All of us know basically what's right and what's best, but none of us ever lives up to those things all the time. Knowing and acknowledging that fact can help us a great deal.

But we have Jesus Christ in our life, and we can ask for His help. Maybe we need to change our way of thinking of what that perfect grandparent is. Perhaps much of our ideal has been established by books or TV programs. Each of us is unique and don't have to fit a stereotype.

In loving our children and grandchildren, we don't necessarily help them by being available at every moment. We help them most by being ourselves and teaching them that they have to cope with all kinds of situations in life.

Every family and every individual is unique. We do our best when we love our children and our grandchildren as sincerely as we know how. We also try to set before them the best example that we can. We acknowledge our failures and our humanity. At the same time we constantly call out to God to make us more like Jesus Christ.

God, I know I'm not a perfect grandparent and I'll never be perfect. But help me to be as loving as I possibly can be. Amen.

Critical Grandparents

> Love is patient and kind; love is not jealous or
> boastful; it is not arrogant or rude. Love does
> not insist on its own way; it is not irritable or
> resentful; it does not rejoice at wrong, but re-
> joices in the right. Love bears all things, be-
> lieves all things, hopes all things, endures all
> things.
>
> 1 Corinthians 13:4–7 RSV

Week 6, Day 3

Forty-year-old Marcia said, "I love my mother, but she is so overly critical of me."

I remember thinking at the time that Marcia had mis-stated the case. I know her mother. Her mother is not a person that I think of as being critical.

Marcia went on to say that her mother continually nags and seems to delight in telling her everything she does wrong—the way she cooks, the way she keeps house, even the way she disciplines the grandchildren. At the same time I think Marcia's mother would be shocked to hear those words.

Agnes, mother of a two-year-old son says, "Every time my mother-in-law talks to me she seems to start every other sentence with, 'I don't mean to interfere, Agnes, but . . .' and then she starts to interfere."

These criticisms come from parents about their par-ents. These problems can be solved. They occur because grown children feel that their parents are constantly finding fault with them.

One problem may be that our children are still look-ing to us for approval. They may not come right out and say, "Dad, am I doing this right?" or "Mother, are you pleased with what I'm doing?" They may, however, send out messages to get you to say that they are doing okay. We may not do things the same way our children do them, but that doesn't mean they're right or wrong. One of the first things we need to do is make sure our children don't take what we're saying as criticism. That requires some real heart searching on our part. Are we criticizing them? Do we really think our way is superior?

When we constantly offer unasked for advice, one of two things generally happens. (1) Our children turn deaf ears to us. Or, (2) our children build up resentment.

Even when we think our children are doing things wrong, remember that everyone is entitled to his/her own share of mistakes. We've made our share, too, and our children are entitled to make theirs. They won't make the same mistakes we made; they'll make their own. If we're a critical parent, it may be that we're trying to be too protective. We're trying too hard to mold our children (and grandchildren) to fit our expectations.

One of the hardest things I had to learn is that my children don't share the same expectations that I do. I had great visions of my firstborn going to college and I had a future all mapped out for her. Instead of going to college, she chose to work and then got married. I learned to accept that it was her life and she can do with it as she chooses. I'm there to love her and support her.

One thing we as parents and grandparents need to remember is the difference between advice and approval. Our offspring may seek advice. Advice is something we offer and they consider and then follow it or not. It's important that we communicate that. It's fine for us to say, "Here's one way of looking at it," or "Here's what I'd do." But we need to let our children know that the choice is theirs.

Approval is different. Our children ask for approval because they need assurance. We need to remind them that they need no approval from anyone except God Himself. When our children constantly need our approval, it speaks of their own immaturity, and we don't help them by continuing to play the game.

When we suspect that we're criticizing our children,

one way we can help is to say, "Now I want to be sure you've heard what I've said. Tell me what you think I just said." If our children repeat it back as criticism, we know they've heard it differently than we've intended.

Think through the words we've spoken. Do they actually speak of or imply disapproval?

Love is not critical. Love does not point fingers. Love says, "I love you regardless of your actions and the way you solve or don't solve your problems."

It might help if we have the courage to do so to say to our children, "Look, sometimes I may get very critical. I don't intend to, but if you think I'm being critical, tell me."

Of course we have to be able to hear when they say, "Yes, you are being critical." What we're trying to do as grandparents is to bring about closer relationships with our children and our grandchildren. One way we learn to do that is to be more loving and less critical.

God, help me to love without being critical of my children. Help me to accept them as different and yet not disapprove. Amen.

Living Now

> I am under obligation both to Greeks and to barbarians. . . I am eager to preach the gospel to you also. . . . I am not ashamed of the gospel.
>
> Romans 1:14–16 RSV

Week 6, Day 4

I admire my older sister Evelyn. She learned to drive when she was fifty-four years of age. That same year she joined the work force and got a good job; ten years later she looks happier and younger than she did when she was forty. She's not only a grandmother; she has recently become a great-grandmother. I think one of the reasons I admire my sister is she's living in the now.

I've always admired that very thing about the writings of the Apostle Paul. He could have written these various letters reminding his readers of past achievements and concentrated on how things used to be. Instead, his letters breathe with what's going on now. In the first chapter of Romans he writes, "I am *now* ready" three times. All through his letters the same message comes through.

As grandparents, and therefore as people who are anywhere from middle-aged to the elderly, our temptation is to look backwards, to forget what's going on now and think only of the good old days or what life might have been.

By contrast, in the story of the Jewish people going into the new land, there's a fellow named Caleb. When they reached the new land he was eighty years old. He's not worried about his age. He says that he is as strong and healthy as when he was a young man. That may have been an exaggeration. He simply meant, "I'm not going to give up and die like all those old people out there. I'm going into the land because I'm still alive."

Living in the now means that we take risks. We don't settle for what we have had in the past. We don't worry about the future. We live in the present. We remind ourselves that because God is alive, life can get better all the time.

People often say, "Life is what we make it." That's right. And one way that we make life enjoyable and happy is by looking at what's going on now and becoming a part of it.

In the famous play by the same name, Auntie Mame becomes such a delightful character because her theme is always, "I want to live!" It's a challenge to the middle-aged and elderly. All through the play up until the very end she's always doing something new and exciting, always finding life fresh.

That's exactly the way God has intended it for His

people. We live in the now. We appreciate the good things going on in our lives as we prepare ourselves for the future. But the future may still be a long way off. Right now all we have is today. Let's enjoy today and make the most of it.

God of all ages and all time, help me not to concentrate on looking backwards nor only on what's ahead. Help me live in the present and make the most of it. Amen.

If Only . . .

Then Joseph brought his father Jacob and presented him to the king. Jacob gave the king his blessing, and the king asked him, "How old are you?" Jacob answered, "My life of wandering has lasted a hundred and thirty years. Those years have been few and difficult, unlike the long years of my ancestors in their wanderings."

Genesis 47:7–9 TEV

Week 6, Day 5

"If only I had not married so young . . ."

"If only I had not quit my job at IBM . . ."

"If only we had not moved to Maryland . . ."

Those are words of regret. One of the disabilities of middle- and older-age people is that we tend to look back and regret the mistakes (or seeming mistakes) that we made earlier in life.

We all make wrong moves—career changes, family decisions, personal choices. We can think about those mistakes, lament them, and wish we had not done it that way. Or we can move on with an eye toward the future

and say, "That's my past and that's the way it happened."

I suspect Jacob lived in his past. He'd been a wicked
fellow. He had cheated his father and deceived his
brother. He had also outsmarted his wily father-in-law.
His cruel sons had tried to kill their brother Joseph. Now
a hundred and thirty years old, Jacob stands before the
king of Egypt. He confesses to the king that his days
have been full of sorrow.

That's where many of us stop. We think back on all
the things that have happened to us and regret them.

A healthy stance in life acknowledges the past which
includes our mistakes and admits there's nothing we can
do about them. That's what is. We can make decisions
and do something about the future, but the past will always be the past. There's nothing we can do to change it.

As a lesson on the past, I think of the poem "Maude
Miller." It's a story about a young farm girl who gives a
nobleman a drink of water. Their eyes meet and love
touches them both. Yet their lives are different, eco-
nomically and socially. Nothing ever comes of that ro-
mantic spark. As the poem ends, both Maude and the
gentleman are now married to different people and
they're reviewing their lives. Both of them think quite
separately what it would have been like if they had married each other. The poem ends, "The saddest words of
tongue and pen, are these, it might have been."

They are sad words. We cannot change the past. We
can only make the most of the future. With Jesus Christ
life can continue to get better.

*Lord God, erase the regrets from my life because there's
nothing I can do about them except ask You to forgive my
failures. Turn my eyes toward You and let me enjoy the
days I have left. Help me make wise choices in all that I
do. Amen.*

"He's Not Here"

"Don't be alarmed," he said. "I know you are looking for Jesus of Nazareth, who was crucified. He is not here—he has been raised! Look, here is the place where he was placed."

Mark 16:6 TEV

Week 6, Day 6

The other day I drove through a section of Atlanta where I used to live. What memories came back in the place of my first congregation, where my children entered into their teen years. As I drove slowly through the area I remembered walking past those same houses with my wife or with one of the children. I saw the house where my son's best friend lived, and another house where one of my daughters used to babysit.

Most of all, I realized that the neighborhood had changed. Perhaps now it was a little more shabby, certainly older. In the five minutes it took to drive down those streets, to look over the neighborhood and relive some experiences, a fact became clear to me: I had only memories left.

I could remember the past and our experiences in that neighborhood, but I couldn't relive any of it. In many ways I'm glad for that. I've grown, life has taken on new directions, and I really don't want to return to that time of life.

On the other hand, my head carries many pleasant memories. It seems to me now that it was very peaceful then and fewer problems. (However, as I think more realistically, life was just as problematic then as it ever is. Our minds select memories, and we tend to shut out the unpleasant.)

Even though we move on in our lives, most of us have periods when we want to go back. Especially we who are grandparents like to remember "good ole days" when life seemed simpler and less complicated. I don't think life really was simpler or less complicated, only different. Our memories have made it seem more beautiful or more simple than it really was. We often want to reclaim the past and move back into it. But we know we can't.

As I think of my attempt to enter into past experiences, it made me think of an incident in Mark's Gospel. Jesus had told His disciples for three years that He was going to die. They didn't believe or else couldn't grasp the implications of what He said. Then the Romans crucified Him. After His death the disciples came to the tomb, only to discover the stone rolled away and no body inside. Mark records that a young man (an angel) met them and said, "Don't be afraid. Jesus, whom you're looking for, isn't here. He's gone."

As grandparents, we need to hear those words—"He is gone."

Perhaps part of the affliction of growing up and being a grandparent is that we want to go back and reclaim the past. Like those disciples, we keep looking for where Jesus used to be. He's not there now. None of us are where we used to be. We've all moved forward.

One of the exciting things about life is that it's always going onward. And as long as we keep going onward, we keep growing.

Eternal God, help me appreciate the past, remember the good things, and yet look forward to the future. Amen.

Lovers Still

> ... Love is as powerful as death; passion is as
> strong as death itself. It bursts into flame and
> burns like a raging fire. Water cannot put it
> out; no flood can drown it. But if anyone tried
> to buy love with his wealth, contempt is all he
> would get.
>
> Song of Songs 8:6, 7 TEV

Week 6, Day 7

The elderly couple sat across from me at a restaurant.
All through the meal I kept looking at them. They were
both gray-headed and, I guessed, probably in their six-
ties. What attracted me was the obvious affection between them. He patted her hand. Once she touched his
cheek. They sat close together and when not actually
eating, they constantly looked at each other.

I was only in my twenties when I saw that couple. At
first it disgusted me. "What are two old people doing
acting like teenagers?" I said under my breath. The
more I watched them, the more fascinated I became.
Here was an elderly couple after many years of marriage
who were still lovers.

A little later I saw them again getting into their car.
She hobbled slightly, and he had his arm around her. He
opened the door and kissed her gently on the cheek before she got inside. Lovers still.

We often forget that when we think of being grandparents, love still endures—that is, if we help it to endure. When we're young and our eyes are filled with
stars, we become aware of the statement made in the
second chapter of Genesis, "A man shall leave his father
and mother and shall be joined to his wife, and the two

shall become one flesh." We think about that during the child-bearing years. We talk of love, passion, togetherness, and sex. But somehow we assume that when people reach the grandparent stage things such as sex, love, and affection become less important. They become less important only if we choose to make them unimportant.

I attended a funeral of an elderly man. He died in his seventies after nearly fifty years of marriage. Several of us were talking together about him. One of them said, "You know what always made me feel so good about him?" Then she answered her own question. "The two of them were still lovers until the time he died. It was always so marvelous to me to watch him walk into a room. No matter how many people were there, he always searched for her. Their eyes would meet in a moment of recognition, and only then would he acknowledge other people's presence."

What a wonderful compliment—they were lovers still, even though grandparents. Grandparents of any age can still be lovers.

God, renew our love and rekindle the fire, because we know that love not only can endure but You meant it to last forever. Amen.

Helpful Hints for Those About to Become Grandparents

1. Be willing to help after the birth of the baby—if asked.
2. The new parents are grown-up adults, not children. They can make their own decisions. They don't need parental interference or intervention, unless they ask for it.
3. Don't compete with the other grandparents by buy-

ing expensive presents or monopolizing the parents' time.
4. Our children have a different perspective from ours. They don't do things as we did. Because they are adults, they have chosen their life-style.
5. When visiting, remember you are a guest in that home (or when they visit you, remember they are guests).
6. You'll love the new grandchild because babies are easy to love. Don't neglect the parents, especially the new mother, who needs help and consideration.
7. Disposable diapers are just as respectable as cloth. Pacifiers won't disfigure a child or destroy his/her character. All this says is that if your grandchild starts out life differently than your children did, it will do no irreparable damage.
8. Babies don't need extra-warm bundling (as many of us were taught).
9. Breast-feeding can be an emotional subject. Find out for yourself the pros and cons, but let the parents decide for themselves.
10. Don't be afraid to say "I don't know," whether you're talking about a two-month-old infant's sudden rash or why Melinda cried out in her sleep.
11. Pray much for the new child, for the new parents, for yourself. Ask God to make this a happy period for all of you.

Helpful Hints on Being a Grandparent

1. Enjoy this time of life. It's a new stage of your own development. You've earned the right to enjoy the little ones.
2. Be loving and available grandparents, as much as

your schedule and life-style permit. But don't be the ubiquitous kind (always underfoot) and constantly offering advice that sounds like marching orders.

3. Learn to listen. Let the grandchild find you as a source of someone who cares, whom he/she can talk to, and yet won't pump for family information.

4. Pray daily for your children and your grandchildren.

5. About giving advice: *don't*. They'll love you for it.

6. Being a grandparent doesn't mean you're over the hill or too old for sex. Grandparents can still be great lovers.

7. Make your home a warm, welcome place which the grandchildren look forward to visiting and are reluctant to leave.

8. As grandparents, we have much to teach—values, attitudes, knowledge. But we can also learn to see life anew through the eyes of the young.

9. When you criticize a child, you're criticizing the parent; when you compliment the child, you're complimenting the parent. That means that most parents (unconsciously) view their offspring as extensions of themselves.

10. Conflicts will occur—even though we love our children and grandchildren. Acknowledge and deal with the conflicts, asking forgiveness when appropriate. Most of all, keep the relationship open.

11. Children aren't miniature adults. When we talk to them, let's use words and concepts on their level.

12. When we grandparents have the responsibility to discipline grandchildren, we need to do it lovingly but firmly. Why not reward children for doing right while minimizing their wrongs? Above all, teach them about God's forgiveness by the way we accept and forgive others.

13. Some *don'ts* to minimize the roadblocks in relationships: Don't urge children to deny their feelings. Don't offer easy solutions and glib answers to life. Don't lecture or moralize. Don't threaten punishment. Don't play psychiatrist.

14. We'll never be *perfect* grandparents; no one ever is. By loving and depending on Jesus Christ for daily strength, we can be *very good* grandparents!
15. Don't stop growing as an individual. Being a grandparent is a new stage of life—not the final one.